Hurry Slowly

Living from the Inside Out

RUDI HARST

*To Kathy —
with gratitude and
blessings,
Rudi*

CELEBRATION CIRCLE
PUBLISHING

Hurry Slowly
Living from the Inside Out

RUDI HARST

Celebration Circle Publishing
1830 East Pyron
San Antonio, TX 78223

Copyright © 2003 by Rudi Harst

Cover Illustration Zet Baer
Cover Design, Interior Illustration Mark Rue
Author Photograph Steve Lewis
Typesetting, Production Judy Bankhead

Library of Congress Control Number: 2003094006

ISBN 0-9742430-0-0
Printed in the United States

Excerpt from Chapter XIV in THE LITTLE PRINCE by Antoine de Saint-Exupery, © 1943 by Harcourt, Inc. and renewed 1971 by Consuelo de Saint-Exupery, English translation © 2000 by Richard Howard, reprinted by permission of Harcourt, Inc.; the chapter *Making Peace with War* © 2002 by Rudi Harst first appeared as an essay in the SAN ANTONIO CURRENT; the poem *Come* was published as lyrics to the song on the music CD by Rudi Harst NOW AND THEN © 1997 by Dancing Man Music; THE PRECIOUS PRESENT by Spencer Johnson © 1984 by Doubleday and Company.

Life is not a puzzle to be solved,
but a mystery to be contemplated.

ANTHONY DE MELLO

Introduction   1

v

Introduction

When faced with the need to make tough choices, it's tempting to rely solely on our rational minds and observable facts to help us make decisions, the way most of our cultural training has taught us to do. But I believe that the heart of the personal growth process lies in a willingness to watch for clues coming from beyond the physical realm as well. This means learning to listen for what some would call the still, small voice of God, or the quiet workings of Spirit. Others might prefer to think of it as being true to our Buddha nature, honoring the wisdom of the Tao, or tuning into the intelligence of intuition.

After many years of investigation, reflection and conversation with others, I've found that it doesn't seem to matter all that much what you call this guiding force or whether you learn about it through prayer, meditation, contemplation or illumination, whether you arrive by way of a joyous, mystical experience or by a painful near-death experience, by a guru's initiation or an alcoholic's desperation. What appears to matter most is a willingness to see beyond the physical plane, to hear with your heart, to live life more deliberately. Even if you're in a hurry, there are ways to "hurry slowly", to become more porous to life. You may not be able to change the pace of life's demands on you right now, but with practice and persistence you can certainly learn to change the pace of your responses.

Of course, this is nothing new. People have long had to wrestle with their choices. But the decision-making process has become significantly more difficult in recent years, due to the rapidly growing number of options we face in our "zoom-zoom" culture. Remember that the human brain and nervous system evolved slowly over millions of years. For much of that time, our choices concerning food, travel, clothing, work and relationships were very limited by what was available in our immediate surroundings. These days, even seemingly simple choices like what to eat for breakfast or what clothes to wear to work involve an array of options that would have been unthinkable for an ordinary person a hundred years ago. And then there are the more difficult choices involving career-changes, relationships, education, economics, politics, child-rearing, aging parents, environmental stewardship and spiritual fulfillment — with a non-stop flow of conflicting advice coming from our families, friends, therapists, TV, radio, magazines and the Internet, to name just a few. Whew!

Meanwhile, the physiological makeup of our relatively slow-paced, nature-based nervous system has changed very little, if at all. Again and again, the voices of our helter-skelter consumer culture urge us to "Just do it!" — but our brains scream back, "Do what? When? How?" No wonder so many of us are feeling stressed, depressed and unable to really rest.

I'm not promising any simple answers here, because I think life is much too full of magic, madness, miracles

2

and messiness to be reduced in that way. Instead, this collection of reflections invites you to explore the person you truly are and who you are becoming. This involves finding ways to hush your monkey mind and listen for that other voice, the smaller, quieter one, the one that whispers softly in the silences between your thoughts, the one that tiptoes over the threshold of your dreams, the one that tugs quietly at the shirt-sleeves of your intuition. It's relatively simple, though seldom easy to hear this small voice through the clamor. It takes time, energy and patience to live from the inside out, and I hope you'll find that this book supports you in the process.

Please note that while most books are meant to be read cover-to-cover, from front to back, this isn't necessarily one of them. These chapters have been arranged by the seasons of the year, with each piece assigned to the season during which it was written. Like most of life's lessons, these writings appear here more or less at random, without any particular chronological order, yet with a rhythm and reason all their own.

winter

Another Dawn, Another Choice

It doesn't happen every morning, but whenever possible I love to get up before the sun rises. It's so delicious to sit in the pre-dawn darkness, listen to the stillness and breathe in the blessings of the new day being born right before my eyes. When I can, I tiptoe out of the house, walk to the end of the block and stand on the riverbank, reading the morning sky like someone else might scan the daily newspaper, hungry for news.

But the news I seek isn't found in the headlines; it's reflected in the skyline, the humidity, the wind, the sounds of the earth stirring. I learn about it while counting stars and gauging clouds, alternately sitting still, writing and moving slowly through the precise choreography of Tai Chi Chuan. It's such a selfish pleasure, I suppose, spending so much time breathing deeply, taking the pulse of the day, making myself available to the flow of spirit. But it feels like the right thing for me to be doing, so here I am once again.

As often happens at this time of year, today the river is covered by a thick blanket of morning fog. It comes curling up off the water, crawling up onto the road where I stand, wrapped in awe and mystery at the sight of this gray, swirling mist. The temperature is in the mid-20s, chillier than it's been in a long time. The cold nips at my nose and toes, so I pull my down jacket a little tighter to my chest, feeling blessed by its snug fit.

Suddenly a sense of expanded awareness reminds me how fortunate I am: I'm out here in the cold by choice. My warm house and a hot breakfast are only a few feet away, unlike the many homeless folks who spent the freezing night huddled beneath trees and bridges all along this same riverfront. Aware, too, that while I'm standing here feeling peaceful, American soldiers are waging a war in Afghanistan, wielding my tax dollars to protect my freedom. Aware that while I'm busy feeling harmony with Mother Earth, my home is being centrally heated by non-renewable fossil fuels, my comfortable clothes probably sewn by underpaid, overworked garment makers in a *maquiladora* in Mexico or Pakistan.

I am not using these thoughts to beat myself up. I'm simply doing my best to focus awareness on the moment at hand while making peace with the many contradictions involved in learning to live mindfully. Taking some quiet time. Attempting to make conscious choices about how I will spend my time, money and energy today. Knowing the power of conscious co-creation, I take this opportunity to set my intentions for the day. It helps to remember the story of a little girl who came home from kindergarten and presented her mom with her latest drawing. When the mom asked how she'd come up with such a beautiful picture, the little girl said, "I just had a think and drew a line around it!"

As the morning sun peaks over the horizon, I can almost hear it asking me, "Why not come up with a new think for today and then draw a life around it?"

Easing into the New Year

There's a wonderful anecdote about a little 6-year-old girl sitting at the circus eating a big, fluffy ball of cotton candy. A well-meaning grownup sitting next to her asked, "What's a little girl like you doing with such a big cotton candy?" The little girl replied seriously, "Mister, I'm a lot bigger on the inside than I look on the outside!" I love that story. It helps me remember that we are all much bigger on the inside than we seem on the outside.

As we enter the New Year we may find ourselves thinking of making a fresh start. Perhaps we're hoping to launch a new project at work, start a diet, stick to a budget, find a more satisfactory type of relationship or open to a deeper level of spiritual living. As laudable and wonderful as any of these goals may be, it's important to be gentle and patient with ourselves and each other. Give it time.

It's so easy to fall under the invisible but relentless pressure to find "quick fix" solutions for almost everything in our lives, from ring-around-the-collar to credit card crunch, from loneliness to flabby waistlines. We're bombarded by advertisements, radio talk show "experts" and self-help authors who present seemingly quick and easy solutions to our personal problems.

Of course, miracles do occur and instant enlightenment is always a possibility. But for most of us, it just isn't going to happen overnight. As Michael Murphy, author and founder of the Esalen Institute, epicenter of

California's personal growth movement since the 1960s, warns, "Our addiction to the quick fix goes against the built-in learning curve that leads to mastery." In other words, if any deep and lasting changes are to occur in our lives, we must be prepared for the long haul. And in order to stick with it, it's helpful to find some way to keep reminding ourselves that we are "bigger on the inside" than we seem, especially in times of trouble, or when we're stuck in a doldrum for long stretches at a time.

That's one of the advantages of being part of a church, support group or other spiritual community. By gathering our collective energies and reflecting our "bigness" for each other, we support ourselves in hanging in there for the long haul. We can do that in many ways: through creative expression, prayers and rituals; through studying, celebrating, hugging and singing together; through sharing our dreams, fears, wisdom and visions; or by simply sitting together in heartfelt silence.

All of these things are helpful, and I'm writing this in hopes that you will use more and more of the support that is available to you throughout the coming year. I'm also writing to remind you (and myself) to take it nice and easy. There's no rush. After all, we're already perfect, whole and complete. We're just in the process of remembering and growing into the perfection that we always have been.

Once upon a Time

The Little Prince by Antoine de Saint-Exupéry is a magical book for children and adults alike, full of fascinating lessons and characters. One of my favorites is the lamplighter who lived and worked on a tiny planet. His job was to light his lamp at dusk and put it out at dawn. However, the planet was spinning more rapidly with each passing year, and eventually each day lasted only one minute. Because the lamplighter always followed orders, he became exhausted from lighting his lamp each minute, then extinguishing it moments later.

"I follow a terrible profession," the lamplighter told the Little Prince. "In the old days it was reasonable. I put the lamp out in the morning, and in the evening I lighted it again. I had the rest of the day for relaxation and the rest of the night for sleep."

"And the orders have not been changed since that time?" asked the Little Prince.

"The orders have not been changed," the lamplighter replied. "That is the tragedy! From year to year the planet has turned more rapidly and the orders have not been changed!"

There are times when I feel much like the lamplighter, rushing like mad to keep up with my to-do list in a world that spins ever faster. Like most of my peers, that's what I was taught when I was growing up: to do all my work, turn it in on time and, if at all possible, get an A+ by doing it perfectly. That was one thing when the task was mowing the lawn or memorizing multiplication tables or writing an essay on Thomas Jefferson. But it's quite something else to try to meet the many conflicting needs and tasks of adult life in a time when the pace of life is accelerating rapidly.

Because "our orders have not been changed," it is all too easy to end a day feeling defeated by the seven important things that we didn't get done, rather than be satisfied and fed by the five or six or even eighteen things we did. So we take time management courses or buy ever larger organizers with more elaborate task-tracking systems. We upgrade our computers so we can fax, e-mail and tap into the vast resources of the Internet and use cellular phones to make use of our driving time to return the ever-increasing flood of phone messages coming in on our pagers. Yikes!

While I admit to having Luddite tendencies, I'm not against the use of appropriate technology, and I may well end up using one or more of these new tools someday. But I'm also clear that they're not the solution to this nagging feeling that trails me (and so many others I know) like a shadow, urging me to go faster, do more, get more done. Because as long as I keep thinking of time as a linear, chronological yardstick which measures my success or failure in discrete units of time and Things Done versus Things UnDone, I'm going to spend much of my life feeling rushed and unsatisfied.

However, so much of this changes each time I remember to open up to Kairos or Spirit Time or the

Eternal Now as often as possible during the course of the day, to breathe deeply, take off my blinders, open my senses and move my attention to the Still Point where everything and nothing occur simultaneously. It's awkward to write or talk about, but it's actually quite a simple thing to do. Not necessarily easy, but simple. Mostly, it's just a matter of sitting or standing still long enough to get centered and view the day's activities without attachment. Seen from this perspective, it's usually much easier to choose what to do next, then give that task focused attention so it gets done more easefully and joyfully. Not only that, but during that time of rest and detachment, I can allow unseen hands and unknown forces to come to my aid and make connections I might never have made myself.

How does it work? I don't know. But I know that it does — not that I've mastered the process by any means. As a matter of fact, one reason I'm writing these words is to reinforce my own behavior, so I remember to do it more often (and perhaps encourage you to do it, too). Then, separately and together, we can go about the business of quietly changing the orders we live by.

What's Cooking?

Zet and I both love to eat well and we enjoy a variety of tastes. We also both love to cook, although we have very different styles of working in the kitchen. I tend to be an improviser and short-order cook who likes the challenge of using whatever ingredients we happen to have on hand to make a quick stew or stir-fry. Usually, my main goal is to make as hearty a meal as possible while getting the food from the fridge to the cutting board to the dinner table in thirty minutes or less.

Zet, on the other hand, really likes to cook more deliberately. She loves to garner new ideas by watching cooking shows or pouring over food magazines and cookbooks to find new recipes. When a menu really strikes her, she'll wait until she has a day when she can shop for the ingredients, then set aside the afternoon and really cook up a delicious storm.

We've learned a lot from each other's cooking over the years. I've learned to appreciate the art of deliberation and she's gotten pretty good at stir-frying. Both styles have their advantages and limitations. I can get food on the table quickly, but my repertoire is limited. Many of the meals tend to taste the same. Zet's meals take more time, but are also more fun to eat, and invariably yield new ingredients and preparation techniques.

I've relayed this information because I think there are some parallels to be drawn to my spiritual life and perhaps yours, too. Given our busy schedules, it's difficult to do much more than meditate for twenty minutes in the morning, with some short prayers or breath work during the course of the day and maybe a few minutes of quiet time before bed. It's not the ideal, but it's enough to feed me on a day-to-day basis, like stir-frys and sandwiches. But periodically, I get hungry for something more. Then I know it's time to set aside a full day to go sit by the river and drink deeply of Mother Earth. Or turn off the phone and spend the day reading and meditating. Or go on a spiritual retreat and explore new territory inside myself. Regardless of the method used, I know I need to give myself the time and space to feed that part of me that can not be fed in any other way.

I'm convinced that while there is no one Right Way to travel the path of Spirit, it is clearly not helpful to ignore the deep hunger for spiritual nourishment that wells up inside of all of us from time to time. It's a matter of paying close attention. So, the question for this moment is, What are you hungry for?

Come

Come to the Light, come to Christ,
come to Krishna, come to Buddha
to the Father and the Mother Goddess, too
come to Allah, come to Jesus,
as the Sacred Spirit frees us
and reminds us who we really are in Truth.

Come you doubters and believers,
come you frightened and confused
come all ye faithful and you faithless ones, come too
come you losers and you winners,
come you would-be saints and sinners
come remember who you really are in Truth.

Come walking tall or on your knees,
come in your fancy clothes or ragged as you please
come wearing hats, or shaved and bald,
come feeling pain or not feeling much at all
but come, don't stay behind, hiding in the shadows
of your mind — come, remember who you are.

Come you givers and you takers
and you very clever fakers
come you heroes and banditos on the run
come you lovers and you liars
and you prisoners of desire
come remember that we really are all One.

Come feeling mad or feeling scared,
come feeling sad because you think nobody cares
come all alone or in a crowd,
come sit in silence or sing it right out loud
but come, don't stay outside, hiding in the fears
you feel inside — come, remember who you are.

Come to the Light, come to Christ,
come to Krishna, come to Buddha
to the Father and the Mother Goddess, too
come to Adonai and Jesus,
as the Sacred Spirit frees us
and reminds us who we really are in Truth.

Come remember who you are.

Dead Ends and Detours

Our house sits on a dead end street. Legend has it that this section of East Pyron Avenue was once part of the original *El Camino Real* or "The King's Highway," which connected all the colonial Spanish missions from the Texas Gulf Coast to California. These days, Pyron is a long street which stretches across much of Southside San Antonio. But this little part of Pyron we live on is just two blocks long, with seven houses located on a thirty acre tract tucked in between some railroad tracks and the San Antonio River. Our neighborhood is such a geographic anomaly that very little traffic comes through and I've come to recognize most of the vehicles that pass our house. All the neighbors' cars usually leave for work by 8:30, the mail truck comes at about 10:00, and garbage/recycling is collected on Tuesdays and Fridays at 3:00. Other than the occasional visitors to our house and the propane delivery truck, that's about it. Except for the people who are lost, that is. They're pretty easy to spot. Not only are they driving unfamiliar cars, they're almost always going way too fast for folks who are only a few yards from encountering the barricade which prevents them from plunging down the riverbank and into the water.

Being a people-watcher by nature, I've made a point of checking out drivers' reactions to encountering this dead end. Some are clearly puzzled by their predicament. They spend a few minutes checking a map or asking directions from a neighbor if they can locate one. But it's interesting to note that most drivers simply do a quick U-turn and, without pausing, zoom back up the street just as fast or faster than they came. It's as if they don't really know where they're going, but they're in a big hurry to get there!

I know that I'm just guessing about what's going on in the heads of those folks. There's also a good chance that I'm projecting my own tendencies onto others. But I suspect that what happens at the end of our street is an apt metaphor for the way many of us react when we find ourselves feeling lost in the course of our daily lives. We imagine that we can take on multiple projects, set goals, establish timelines, fill our calendars with appointments, and then zoom around trying to get from Point A to Point B as quickly as possible, preferably in a straight line. But life doesn't always work that way. It turns out that no matter how organized we get or how much we might plan, it's virtually impossible to avoid the delays, detours and dead ends that spring up along the road of life. So what do we do when we find ourselves in such a situation? Instead of taking some time to reassess our location and/or the direction we're headed, we tend to stay in motion, pretending we can just drive right past our feelings of lostness. It's as if working harder and moving faster will get us there more quickly, even if we're not quite sure where "there" is.

The good news is that we always have the option of changing our perception of whatever situation we find ourselves in. How? By stepping into a higher level of consciousness. Taking some time to see ourselves and our situation from a *metaphysical* (beyond the physical) perspective, we make it possible for miracles to happen — miracles being nothing more than wonderfully unexpected events that we can't explain with logic. Perhaps we'll discover that previously unseen helpers were right there waiting to help us all along. Perhaps we'll learn that the detour we encountered wasn't a detour at all, but just a more appropriate route than the one which we'd planned. Perhaps we'll find that the pause itself is what we really needed; just a little time to stop and refresh our soul. Or maybe, just maybe, we'll see that the best solution is to let go of our need for a solution, allowing ourselves to see the situation as being just fine the way it is!

I have no problems,

no enemies — only teachers

whose lessons I have been resisting.

Life is Not a Dress Rehearsal

My aunt recently retired after working many years as an administrative assistant at the Royal Dutch Conservatory of Music in The Hague. Every year, this prestigious music school receives many more applicants than it can accept. Part of my aunt's job was to schedule and coordinate auditions for would-be students from all over the world. She told me that after years of watching these performances, one of the professors demonstrated that he could predict quite accurately which musicians would pass their auditions before they had performed a single note, simply by watching the way they opened their instrument cases and picked up their instruments. His theory was that the care, confidence and respect with which musicians handle their instruments are direct reflections of the way they perform with them.

Being a professional musician myself, I find her story fascinating. I can just imagine how many of those eager applicants spent hours nervously trying to decide which audition piece to perform, which interpretation would impress the judges, or what clothes to wear. How many would have guessed that in the long run the outward appearances of such details really don't matter as much as do the attitude and the spirit with which they are approached? How many would have guessed that the sound of the music they make is a reflection of something much larger than mere musicianship?

Her story reminds me that life is not a dress rehearsal. I would do well to spend less time rehearsing and worrying about the details of my life and instead pay more attention to my purpose for being who, what and where I am. As I focus on my purpose, I am connected to the bigness of who I really am (I AM) and to the power of The Source, through which all things are possible and all challenges (even auditions) can be successfully met. It's also important to remember that connecting with my purpose is not merely a mental exercise. Rather, it requires me to invest myself fully at the feeling level (what some would call the Soul Level), to turn inward and allow my heart to be filled with the kind of bigness and boldness that creates possibilities.

Does that sound too scary? Too airy-fairy? Does it seem too complex? Something only someone else can do, someone more talented or well-trained than you? That's not true. It's actually a very natural and straightforward process, something most of us knew as children but have long since forgotten. We're simply in the process of remembering.

Gathering with like-minded individuals is helpful to me and many others, especially in a worship setting. The conscious use of music, meditation, ritual, art, prayer and poetry can help us remember and rediscover who we really are and why we're really here. They are powerful tools, but they are not the work itself. That work can only be done by you and I as individuals, turning inward, one moment, one breath, one choice at a time. Unfortunately, it's something we all have to do for ourselves; fortunately, we don't have to do it alone. Look around. On this path of remembering, there are so many of us walking alone together.

Brushed by an Angel

From time to time, people ask me how I got started on this spiritual path which has become my passion as well as my profession. Usually I deflect the question, muttering something about it having been a complicated process that couldn't really be explained. But recently, I spent some time reflecting on that question and realized that there was one day — actually, one particular moment — when the clouds in my heart parted and a light came shining through. It happened in October 1979. I was a twenty-seven-year-old professional musician whose life was sputtering, personally and professionally. In a few short months I'd moved back to San Antonio from Europe feeling defeated, gotten divorced from my high-school sweetheart, lost my recording contract, and lived through some serious binging on "sex, drugs and rock-n-roll." Broke, sad and scared, I knew I'd hit bottom and that it was time to try a different approach to life, although I had no idea what that might look like. Earning enough to eat and pay the next month's rent was definitely a priority, so when a new friend offered me a job with his house painting company, it seemed like a good idea. I'd never painted professionally before, but since I really needed the cash and had once painted my apartment, I gently exaggerated the story of my experience and got hired.

When I showed up at the jobsite the next day, the

crew was already in the process of painting a beautiful two-story Victorian home in San Antonio's historic King William neighborhood. After briefly introducing me to the woman who was the foreman and the rest of her crew, the boss took one look at the heavy leather gloves I was wearing to protect my guitar-playing fingers, accurately assessed my inexperience with painting, and dispatched me to brush a primer coat in an unobtrusive spot on the rear wall of the second floor. He assured me that it was a safe spot to practice my technique, with only one caveat: "Whatever you do, don't spill any paint on the antique cedar shingle roof covering the porch below."

Sure enough, within minutes, a whole quart of paint squirted out of my gloved hand and landed with a splat on the shingles below. I don't know what I said, but whatever it was, I said it loudly enough that the crew foreman came scrambling up the ladder lickety-split. I was so sure she would get mad and fire me on the spot that I was floored when instead her actual response was a warm, accepting smile and a cheerful offer to help me clean up the mess. She remained friendly throughout the process, even though it took us the rest of the morning to get all the paint off. When noon finally arrived, it only seemed fair to buy her lunch at a nearby restaurant. Conversation came easily. We discovered many mutual interests. She was an artist, too. She'd recently quit her job as a high school teacher and ended a long-term relationship. She also was at a crossroads in her life. Before the day was over we'd become good friends. Before the month was over we were best friends. Since neither one of us was interested in dating or getting involved in another relationship, we didn't have to deal with any of the usual male/female courtship issues. We simply enjoyed each other's company, spending more and more time together. I'd never known anyone like her before. Zet was so kind, so warm, so easy to be with. Within two months we'd managed to fall in love after all and she had become my business partner. We got married on the Summer Solstice of 1981 — and recently celebrated our twentieth anniversary.

So what does all this have to do with my spiritual path? With the benefit of hindsight, I now see that the kindness and acceptance that shone out of Zet's eyes in her immediate reaction to my messy mistake was a doorway into another world. It was a place of trust, a place of peace. Once I'd crossed that threshold and experienced the healing power of unconditional love, there was no turning back. Step by step, I was drawn into a new way of being, learning from various teachers and teachings to see myself and all others as whole, complete and perfect manifestations of the Divine. Of course, it hasn't been all peaches and cream. Zet and I have certainly seen our share of personal and professional challenges. But when difficulties arise, we choose to face them alone together, remembering to maintain our connection to our deepest selves and to our Source.

And why am I telling you this? Because I believe that all of us are always surrounded by people, places and powers that are ready, willing and able to help us find our way, no matter what the circumstances. Our eyes may or may not be able to see our would-be helpers, but our hearts surely can, if we are willing to honor the power of our feelings. I know, because I've been blessed to experience many similar "miracles" since that first magical meeting with Zet. I'm doing my best to stay open to the possibilities of more such encounters and invite you to do the same.

Valentines

Sitting side by side
they stare off into space together separately.

Their words come easily when needed,
but silence, too, lands softly and simply
in the spaces between their reading chairs.

The dimples dancing on her cheeks
are reflected in his laughing eyes.

Hearts speaking clearly without saying a word,
these are the trophies of a long-lasting love
that has laughed and cried and asked, *Why not?*
and listened, waiting in the dark,
for answers that do not always come.

Two partners tied by a knot that holds them without binding
they are still finding their way together and alone:
sometimes he gets lost,
sometimes she gets tired,
sometimes they both forget
to roll up the car windows on a rainy night
and their seats feel cold and wet the next morning.

But mostly the words come easily when needed
and silence, too, lands softly in the spaces between them
side by side
in their reading chairs.

Another Awkward Apology

Despite my very best intentions
and many years of training,
I strain with the feelings behind my words.

They get mixed up
with all those random bits of old habit patterns
trapped in the abandoned basement of my guts
rotting beneath piles of clumsy words
and what comes out gets heard as being hurtful.

What I want to convey gets lost in the shuffle
your feathers get ruffled
I huff and puff and try to act tough
you shy away in silence.

So now my words of apology come wobbling through the air
written on the wings of a paper airplane
that almost flies straight
with high hopes of starting over

— again.

NOTE: You might try this technique the next time you find yourself
at the tail end of an argument with someone you love. Breathe. Wait.
Write your new thoughts on a clean sheet of paper. Fold it. Fly it. Let
it fall where it may. It probably can't hurt, and it just might help.

Living Large

I love going to the movies. It's wonderful to gather in the darkened theater, huddled around the "celluloid campfire", collectively watching drama unfolding on the flickering screen. Cast in the age-old tradition of storytelling, movies have a marvelous capacity for lifting our spirits, reminding us of our connections to ourselves and each other. This capacity is made even more compelling by dazzling new techniques in cinematography, sound and special effects that pull us right into the middle of the on-screen action.

However, it's important to remember that the stories people tell each other have a strong influence on how they define themselves and their own behaviors. It's unfortunate that so many of the current Hollywood films are full of graphic violence, foul language and adrenaline-pumping plot lines. I know I risk sounding like some self-righteous moral conservative, but I'm not. The way I see it, I'm just being practical. After all, our society has to live with the consequences of showing and telling each other such gory stories.

We're already subjected to so much stress merely by being alive in these fast-paced times. So, why pay good money to sit in a theater to absorb additional stressful energy? Numerous studies have clearly shown that physiologically our adrenal and nervous systems can't differentiate between real and imaginary danger. The cycle of tension and release which we undergo while seated in the theater may well serve to get our minds off our real-life woes — but at what cost?

Still, you don't have to be a spiritual seeker to know that a well-told story on the big screen can be a powerful way to connect with the Big Picture of Life at a deeply emotional, mental and spiritual level. The same cinematic wizardry that can leave us feeling tiny and alone can also be used to help us feel extra-large and sublimely connected to the All. And that's precisely why *Simon Birch* is high on my list of favorite movies. Based on John Irving's novel *A Prayer for Owen Meany*, the movie provides a smart, funny, wistful and moving look at some of the all-time Big Questions: "Why do accidents happen? Is there such a thing as an accident or does everything happen on purpose, according to some Higher Plan? And if so, what is my purpose?"

Movies that dare to ask such big questions often wind up drowning in a sticky-sweet pool of sentimentality and/or tripping clumsily over easy answers. *Simon Birch* manages to skirt both of these problems, primarily because of the highly believable performances which the likeable oddball Simon (Ian Michael Smith) and his best friend, Joe (Joseph Mazzello), bring to this screen adaptation of Irving's story.

Smith is a first-time actor, cast because of his diminutive and distinctive body type. But he's a natural. With a soft and sensitive touch, he reminds us that we're all oddballs of one sort or the other, which is to say that we're all unique, and that our uniqueness matters.

If you haven't seen this movie, please consider renting the DVD — partly because I think it's important to provide positive feedback when Hollywood makes such a wonderful movie, but mostly because you deserve to remember how unique you are. Your uniqueness makes a difference in the world when you let it.

Anger's Gift

The arrival of our newborn son, Mateo, was a dream come true for Zet and me. I'll spare you the details, but suffice it to say that he is the answer to a prayer that we had been carrying in our hearts for 15 years. Mateo is almost a month old now, and the past four weeks have been filled with miracles and wonders, joy and thanksgiving. We are especially grateful for the incredible amount of love and support we have received from our friends and extended family in the Circle. The outpouring of gifts, cards, letters and blessings has been a magnificent experience of abundance for us all. Mateo has literally been showered with love.

The name we gave our son is derived from the Hebrew name for Matthew, meaning "gift from God," which he clearly is. But as is so often the case with God's gifts, this one came complete with unforeseen, uncomfortable consequences. Sure, I'd been warned about the sleepless nights and the dirty diapers, the high bills and the low energy. That the carefully tended dynamics of my long term love affair with Zet would change literally overnight. But what I personally hadn't counted on was the mixed feelings that arrived in my heart the moment that Mateo arrived in our house. Along with joy came deep jealousy. With hope for the future came ferocious fears of failure. Scariest of all were the wild waves of red hot anger which arose in my heart during the late, late nights of the second and third weeks, when the elation had worn off and the reality of sleep deprivation began to set in. On two separate occasions, I found myself feeling furious when he wouldn't eat or sleep or stop fussing for what seemed like hours on end. Each time I was shocked by feeling so deeply alone in my own anger, confused by the clear evidence that after all these years of prayer and meditation I would still be capable of such deep rage toward such a tiny, lovable being. And it didn't help matters any that during the daylight hours I was being inundated with congratulations and heartfelt assurances of what great parents Mateo had chosen. Such compliments only increased the extent to which my need to perceive myself as a peaceful, loving man clashed with the stark presence of these late night bouts of anger.

The third time this happened in the middle of the night, I really panicked. I found myself feeling so angry with Mateo's behavior, so trapped in the role of failed father, so wrapped up in my desperate need to control the uncontrollable, that I trembled with rage, choking back screams, wanting to shake him the way that he had shaken me to the very roots of my being. Fortunately, Grace kicked in before my muscles did. For a moment, time was suspended, framed in a Hollywood-style slow motion sequence in which I could see how close I'd come to violating my son's body, how easily his beautiful softness could have been shattered. Ugly fantasies came swirling through my mind: the baby's limp body; my remorse, the police arrest, the imagined newspaper headlines, the prison sentence, the ruined lives...

In the stunned silence that followed my panic, there was only one thing I could do: surrender. To sit in silence, simply observing my anger long enough to be able to feel my feelings fully, without shame, blame, or judgment. To remember that these feelings of rage, too, are a Divine Gift to be accepted, learned from and released. Breathing deeply, I experienced what I can only call Grace. The fullness of love for Mateo, myself and all of Life came flooding through my body, mind and Spirit. At the very same time flashes of my own childhood memories came visiting, too: haunting reminders of old hurts, fears and temper tantrums; visions of my parents' faces red and twisted with the fear and anger they too must have wrestled with all those years ago, as they struggled to raise six sons under trying circumstances.

I wish that I could report that a Guiding Angel appeared that night, delivering a Twelfth Insight which has altered my life forever. But it wasn't nearly that clearcut or dramatic. It's just that after a few minutes of prayer and meditation, I began to feel the peace sitting in the middle of the turmoil in the middle of my heart. As I became peaceful again, Mateo settled down, too. Eventually we both fell asleep and rested long enough to start over fresh.

Since then, I have noticed a significant shift in my feelings for my son. I now know for a fact the he and I are both strong, willful males, and that it's seldom going to do me much good if I try to out-willpower him. It can only be a losing proposition for one or both of us. I'm fully aware that all of my bright ideas about parenting are changing shape rapidly now that I'm faced with having to make life-affirming, split-second decisions daily. And it's tricky to find just the right balance between setting firm boundaries and allowing Mateo to express himself. But I figure that if I can just remember to treat him with as much love and respect as I claim for myself, he and I will thrive together. And to the extent that I remember to treat others the same way, we'll all benefit. Meanwhile, I'm grateful for anger's gift, as well as all the other blessings that Mateo has brought into our lives.

Safe from the Fallout

Once upon a time,
we were told to find our way to a fallout shelter,
to "duck and cover" our way to safety under classroom desks
in the event of a nuclear attack.

Now we know that if even one warhead
had landed at just one of the several military targets
around this city, there would have been no place to hide
for long enough to matter.

Somehow we survived that time.

But now, holding my newborn son,
still innocent in his nakedness, I wonder
how can I raise him safe from the fallout of the bombs
which are exploding among us –
silently, profitably, relentlessly?

Far more deadly
than anything the Communist arsenal ever contained,
these bombs are quietly killing our children from the inside out
leading them to starve themselves, cheat their friends,
shoot each other down on their own school playgrounds.

The missiles are fired daily
from the bowels of Wall Street and Hollywood,
urging us to feed our children sugar, white flour
and caffeine for breakfast,
toxins, preservatives and grease for lunch and dinner –
filling their souls with endless hours of TV and video games,
clothing their bodies in trendy shoes and clothes
manufactured by virtual slaves in third world sweatshops –
all in the name of free trade and progress.

I want so much to show my son
other possibilities in his lifetime,
but find myself wondering what difference it would make.
With the advertising bombs pounding our eyes, ears,
minds and hearts day in, day out,
how can we shelter ourselves from the fallout
for long enough to matter?

It's easy to ask these hard questions;
much harder to live the answers –
one day,
one meal,
one purchase at a time.
But this is an altar, not a complaint.
A prayer of thanks, given in advance,
for all the support my son has received
and will receive
from his neighbors, friends and family
as we live in our questions, today and tomorrow.

Making Peace with War

Perhaps it would have been different if I'd been living in New York or Washington, D.C. at the time. But for me, the events of 9/11 seemed fairly far off and surreal. As violent and destructive as the airplane attacks were, I was more deeply affected by my fellow Americans' fearful reactions than by the terrorists' actions. It wasn't until two days later that the swirling storm of stories and images really began to penetrate my heart. But when it did, things became very personal in a hurry, taking form in a moment which still echoes through my soul today.

It happened at about 6:30 p.m. on September 13th. I was desperately trying to get to the Mennonite Church before 7:00, where I was scheduled to perform at an interfaith peace service sponsored by the PeaceCenter. I'd agreed to sing at this particular event two months earlier, fully expecting it to be another uplifting, yet depressingly familiar peace rally attended by the same small group of faces I've been seeing at such events for years. But 9/11 had changed everything. I was pretty sure the church would be packed this time, giving our community a much needed opportunity to explore alternatives to the belligerent flag-waving and chest-thumping which had engulfed our nation for the past two days. In short, I was very eager to get there and speak my piece about peace.

Unfortunately, our two-year old son, Mateo, didn't share my enthusiasm. He didn't want to stop playing, finish eating or have his diaper changed — and he sure as heck didn't want to be rushed into leaving the house. My wife, Zet, was busy elsewhere. We hadn't found a baby-sitter, and the only option was to take Mateo with me, whether he liked it or not. He began crying as soon as we got in the car, accelerating into a full-blown temper tantrum before we'd driven two blocks.

In keeping with the policy Zet and I had agreed on long before, I pulled the car over to the curb, turned around in my seat, tried to stay calm and distract him. No luck. More screaming. Time running short. To heck with our family policy. I drove on, tempers running high on both sides of the car. Then he pulled a real no-no. He threw a toy at me. I immediately slammed on the brakes, pulled into a parking lot, jerked open the back door and started screaming at the top of my lungs, demanding his cooperation. All my frustration came spilling out, filling the car with rage. That sure showed him. It scared him quiet, lips quivering, eyes fearful, not another peep. Mission accomplished, I slammed the door shut and headed back to my side of the car. Suddenly the violence and foolishness of my actions came echoing through my heart. I stood stock-still, stunned by the realization that with my tongue, I'd beaten and bruised my beloved boy into submission just as certainly as if I had attacked him with a baseball bat. And why? Because I was in a hurry to get to a peace rally where I could urge others to explore non-violent responses to violence!

It was pretty silly and I would have laughed, except I was feeling far too foolish and pathetic. Climbing into the back seat, I begged Mateo to forgive me. But looking into his beautiful, dark sad eyes I could immediately see that remorseful apologies wouldn't suffice. What he and I were both hungering for was the experience of peace. So we simply sat there together in silence for a long minute or two. Feeling our feelings, looking at each other with love, finding what comfort we could. Not for long, but long enough, I suppose. The storm passed.

The service was well underway by the time that we finally found a parking space and wound our way through the overflowing crowd, just in time for me to take my turn at the microphone, where I introduced my song by relating the incident in the car. I was able to make light of it, and the audience laughed with me. But the lesson was plain to see, and there was nothing funny about it, then or now. For in that painfully transparent moment, it became clear to me that somehow we must learn to change our ways, as individuals, as nations, as a planet. We cannot make peace by subduing others with threats, jets, or bigger better bombs. Whether a war breaks out in the family car or on a far-off battlefield, everyone always loses. Peace is more than just the absence of violence. It is an active, ongoing process which requires mutual respect, reconciliation and communication instead of confrontation. Anything less is just another mess waiting to happen in the form of the next shouting match, the next line scratched in the desert sand between two armies, the next big attack on our survival as a species.

Shark's Teeth

One day an atheist went fishing off the Gulf Coast. It was a hot day, and he wasn't catching much, so he decided to go for a dip. After swimming a while, he saw a shark circling around, getting closer and closer. There was no one else around, his boat was too far to reach, and he was feeling mighty helpless. Just as the shark got close enough to open his terrifying jaws and attack, the atheist screams, "Oh, God, save me!"

Instantly, the shark froze, the clouds parted, and a bright white light shone down from above. The man heard the deep, loud voice coming from nowhere, saying, "You are an atheist; you don't believe in me. Why do you call upon me now?" Too scared and confused to argue, the man agreed, "That's true, I don't believe in you. But how about the shark? Can you make the shark believe in you?"

God replied, "As you wish," and the light retracted back into the heavens. In the silence that followed, the man was shocked to see the huge shark close its eyes, bow its head and say, "Thank you, God, for this food which I am about to receive!"

Sure it's a silly story. But it illustrates the idea that each of us has been given the gift of free will, of choosing what we want to believe and how we will act on our beliefs at any given moment. We can pick from any number of spiritual traditions and/or guidelines to help us make these choices. The questions are: How do we learn to apply spiritual principles to the many choices we're being bombarded with? How can we take a head full of good-sounding ideas and ground them in the soil of our everyday lives? How can we draw from the wisdom of the ages and make a difference in the situation at hand right now?

Having searched along several different paths over the years, I've come to believe that it's mostly a matter of paying attention. Although it's important to listen to our teacher(s) and ask for guidance from the Higher Power of our understanding, it is also essential to let the seemingly ordinary people and circumstances of our daily lives teach us. It is there that Spirit is reaching out to touch us, if only we will let it.

For instance, some of my friends have been gently teasing me for focusing so many of my recent writings and Sunday morning talks on topics relating to my young son, Mateo. They joke that I'm getting obsessed with parenthood. To that, I'm pleased to plead guilty as charged, simply because I'm learning so much from him and the circumstances he brings into our lives. And why not? After all, Zet and I have made a conscious commitment to focus our lives on co-creating a loving, nurturing environment for Mateo, our community and ourselves. That's our priority and where we've chosen to invest the majority of our time and energy for the foreseeable future. It's only natural that much of our spiritual food, and many of our lessons, will come out of this matrix of concerns.

I believe that consciously or unconsciously we set our priorities, then proceed to invest our energy in manifesting them. Whatever we've chosen to focus on, whether it's a career, relationship, health, prosperity or anything else, will show us, teach us what we need to learn in order to grow, but only if we're paying attention. At times, the lessons seem soft and sweet as a baby's smile. At other times, they feel hard and sharp as shark's teeth. That's just how it is. As psychologist Dr. Wayne Dyer is fond of saying, "Pain is inevitable; suffering is optional." The important thing is to release as many of our judgements as possible, remembering that only good will come of our willingness to trust our process, whether it feels comfortable or not. Like the fisherman, we are always free to choose our beliefs and reactions — and peace is always an option.

spring

Taking a Spring Break

Winter's behind us and spring is signaling her warmth in many wondrous ways. The birds, bees, trees and breezes are all doing their part to get our attention: "Hello, humans! Go outside — breathe, listen, watch! Remember, there's more to the world than what you can see from your window, your car, your computer screen. Go outside and touch, smell, feel some of that moreness!"

Having only been in this new home for a year now, I have a long list of things that need to be done in and around the house itself. But that will just have to wait a while longer, because it's clearly time to take off my winter sweater, pick up a spade, and start turning the soil in the garden. A desk-jockey by trade and a city boy by temperament, it's taken me many years to understand the importance of balancing my spiritual and mental work with periodic doses of dirt under my fingernails and sweat in my armpits. Reluctantly at first, to be sure. But now I find it deliciously satisfying to pull weeds and plant seeds. To stick my shovel into the hard-packed earth, turn it over and watch the crumbling black soil come tumbling out teeming with life forms. Mateo loves it, too. Working side by side in the yard with him is one of the most satisfying things I've ever done in my life. He's almost three now, and he's gotten pretty good at digging with his little shovel. Like me, his enthusiasm for gardening often outweighs his skill, but it doesn't seem to matter much. The important thing, as he seems to be trying to show me, is just to be outdoors getting in touch with the world around us.

Fortunately, he's quite patient, pointing to the same uninteresting-looking dirt clod over and over again, until I finally manage to see the ladybug underneath it. "Look, look!" he says, bursting with excitement when he digs up the one special smooth rock that fits just right into his jeans pocket. Placing his forefinger to his lips, he leans over to whisper, "Shh, Papa, the caterpillar is sleeping." I try my best to slow down, watch more closely and match his level of wonder, but I fall short all too often.

"That's okay, take your time. There's no hurry," the soil seems to say as it slips through my fingers. "Soon enough your body will die and come to lie here with the weeds and the worms. Like it or not, you, too, are part of this mysterious, ceaseless cycle of decay and renewal. Learn it now or learn it later. Might as well take a break, take a breath and enjoy this moment in the sun with your son. Take your time..."

Having heard this invitation myself, I'm taking the liberty of extending it to you. Won't you take some time today, tomorrow or sometime sooner than later to go outside and let the waves of spring energy wash through you for an hour, a day, or just a few minutes? Gardening or hiking or biking or simply standing still in a space that lets the Sacred brush your face and feel your place in the circle of life? Whatever, whenever, wherever you take your Spring Break, I trust you'll find yourself feeling renewed, re-energized and reminded of what a power-full person you really are!

Daylight Savings Time

I wake up grumpy, stumbling out of bed as I fumble for my alarm clock. Why is it already so light this morning? Grumbling to myself, I remember that this is the result of switching back to Daylight Savings Time (DST). What I can't seem to remember is exactly what it is we're supposed to save by scooting our clocks back and forth twice a year. It surely isn't sleep!

I'm fairly certain that I'm not the only one out of sorts over this issue. Not the only one whose body rhythms get disoriented by having to deal with these semi-annual wrinkles in time. We humans are creatures of habit, after all. And, since most of our lives are tied to the relentless cadence of the time clock in one form or the other, this hiccup in our bio-rhythm is no laughing matter.

Perhaps you disagree, thinking these time changes are mere inconveniences, not really worth worrying about. Or perhaps your bio-rhythms are simply more flexible than mine are. Still, I find DST to be another symptom of our culture's disturbing trend toward treating our bodies as mere machines, without much regard for the potential consequences. In acquiescing to these semi-annual tugs on our inner clockworks, we take on the characteristics of robots whose inner rhythms can be moved to and fro without regard for the reactions we might have to such disruptions.

We humans seem to have developed a strange sort of

49

short-sightedness during the post-industrial era. For too long we have bulldozed mountains, polluted waters and decimated wildlife at will, pretending that there will be no major consequences for disturbing the wholeness or integrity of the environment. Now, as the bills are coming due, we are gradually coming to see the error of our ways. Could it be that we're submitting ourselves to the same kinds of relentless manipulations we've been inflicting on our ecology? Are we treating our bodies as interchangeable units that can be knocked off schedule *en masse* without considering the consequences?

And why have we embraced DST? Supposedly because we consume less energy that way — a claim that I find both questionable and lamentable. Questionable because our energy-guzzling society clearly doesn't care all that much about saving energy anyway, regardless of how often we mumble to ourselves about the need to conserve resources. Lamentable because this calculation was undoubtedly made by a team of engineers who counted only the BTUs consumed by buildings, lamps and automobiles without considering the costs and quantities of the human energy involved.

Can the amount of fuel saved by turning a city's street lights on one hour later really be equated with the extra energy a single working parent expends to get the kids awake, dressed and off to school an hour earlier than their little bodies want to be awakened? Has anyone ever stopped to calculate the human costs involved to the millions of families involved in such a monumental shift in body rhythms? And just how many productive man-hours of labor are lost when workers' bodies show up for their shift on time while their minds are still trying to catch that extra hour of sleep?

Proponents of DST counter that this is a simple-minded argument, not much different from the concerns of post-World War I era farmers who worried that switching to DST would cause their crops to get burned by too much sun. Supposedly such anecdotal evidence doesn't measure up to the quantifiable statistics provided by utility companies. And that's precisely what I find so lamentable. Who says statistics are more valid or valuable than our individual stories, needs, and desires? And what messages are we sending our children when we tell them that "fitting in with the schedule" of the economy is more important than what their bodies tell them about sleeping and eating? Isn't it bad enough that our lives are so closely tied to the clock without being jerked around like marionettes twice a year?

I say it's time to leave our clocks alone. Daylight Savings Time may have become a given in our schedules, but it can be taken away, too. It is a relatively recent invention after all. It was first introduced early in the twentieth century and only came into widespread usage in America as a result of the OPEC-induced oil shortage in the mid-70s. While it's clear that we need to re-think our culture's addiction to fossil fuels and to find other ways to power our engines, I believe that submitting ourselves to these "hiccups in time" is part of the problem, not the solution. Can't we turn back the clock on the idea of moving our clocks back and forward twice a year?

Receiving a Summons

Having been summoned to Jury Duty, I'm sitting in the Central Jury Room at the courthouse along with several hundred other Bexar County residents. Looking around, I see that we're an amazingly diverse cross section of the populace, all waiting to find out which of us will be impaneled to serve on juries this week. I find it particularly interesting to eavesdrop on the folks lined up in front of the judge requesting exemption from jury duty for various reasons. I try to avoid being judgmental, but some of those requests sound pretty bogus to me. I'm also hearing a lot of grumbling and grousing from others sitting around me: how inconvenient this is, how long we've been kept waiting, the inefficiency of the system and generally wishing they were somewhere besides here.

Now I admit that I'm not all that eager to serve on a jury myself. I have a very busy week planned and it would be a drag to have to re-schedule things — not to mention how expensive it is for a self-employed person like me to lose multiple working days with only a $6 *per diem* compensation. I don't have any corporate comp time or paid vacation days to draw on. But the fact remains that we have been summoned here to fulfill one of our basic duties as citizens. And, whatever its flaws, the trial-by-jury is the cornerstone of our legal system. So here we sit, waiting to fulfill our duties.

I'm saddened to note how many of us are eager to

avoid that duty, if at all possible. It reminds me of an interview with the Russian author and political dissident Aleksandr Solzhenitsyn shortly after he sought asylum in the United States during the 1980's. Asked to comment on the differences he'd noticed between Soviets and Americans, he said something to the effect that he found Americans were quick to claim their rights where Soviets were more apt to talk about their responsibilities.

As I reflect on this, I'm aware of a similar tendency among spiritual seekers in general (myself included). We readily turn to our God/dess for comfort in times of trouble or confusion, just as we look to spiritual leaders, self-help books, seminars and support groups for positive feelings and/or words of wisdom to make us feel good. Yet, how few of us are willing to assume the responsibility of actually living our metaphysical truths day-in and day-out? How many of us are willing to allow ourselves the time for a consistent practice of prayer, meditation and simply listening (which, as far as I can tell, is the central duty we have been asked to undertake on the spiritual path)? Not that I'm trying to place a metaphysical guilt trip on anyone. If my spiritual journey has taught me anything, it is to do my best to keep from placing guilt, shame or blame on myself or anybody else. Instead, I prefer to focus on the power of loving awareness.

So, as I sit in this jury selection room surrounded by bored and restless-acting people, I'm focusing on my gratitude for this moment. Feeling love for myself and everyone around me, I breathe and give thanks for this lesson from Spirit: THIS IS IT! This moment is the Real Thing, not just a dress rehearsal for another Real Life that I'll lead once I leave the courthouse today. All I'm asked to do at this moment, and all I'm inviting you to do as you read these words, is to be aware of some of our responsibilities, and to wear them as appropriately and lightly as possible.

Desk Top

A clock, three photos of loved ones, an unlit candle,
a telephone, small cassette recorder
and a cupful of pens and pencils
standing guard over a row of file folders, neatly stacked
and waiting for action.

This is my desk, my home, my bunker,
where I hunker down and face the world.

My wife walks by, getting her morning in gear.
I see her fill the corners of my eye without watching.
We are detaching from each other after all these years —
bringing us even closer together,
waving hello from our two separate hilltops,
saying good-bye without speaking a word.

In the morning stillness, the air weighs nothing.
Her steps are silent on the cool hardwood floor.

The Donkey with No Riders

I don't know about you, but sometimes I feel like I'm in danger of drowning in the torrents of information and advertising that seem to flow through our household daily. Even though Zet and I usually go for weeks at a time without watching TV, the information still comes pouring into our lives from a multitude of other sources: e-mail, radio, Internet, faxes, newspapers, phone calls, billboards, books, movies, magazines, and ever more cleverly niche-marketed junk mail. Recently, I've noticed I can't even fill my car with gasoline without having to listen to a perky voice inside the gas pump (!) suggest that my day will be much better if I go into the Gas 'n' Guzzle to buy a mega-sized mug of coffee and a donut for only 99 cents.

The problem is that we humans, like most other animals, are genetically hard-wired to be aware of all the incoming information from our environment. This trait enabled our ancestors to make split-second, life-or-death decisions about reacting to things like a movement in the shadows: Was that sound made by a friend or foe, a leaf or a lion? But I believe that this same valuable survival mechanism which has been alerting us to occasional, potential dangers for thousands of years is now causing many of us to feel overwhelmed by the sheer volume of incoming information, especially since much of it is scientifically designed to catch our eye and get our attention. Faced with this non-stop stream of semi-subliminal advice on what to fear, flaunt, wear, want, drink and think, is it any wonder that so many of us spend so much of our time feeling uncertain about who we are and what we really should be doing?

In reflecting on this syndrome, I'm reminded of an old folktale about a farmer and his young grandson who were riding to market on their donkey. It was a beautiful day, and they were as happy as could be. Then as they passed a group of farmhands working in a field, one of the workers said loudly to the others, "Look at those two. They should be ashamed of themselves, both of them riding that poor little donkey. Don't they know that they're much too heavy for that little beast?"

Upon hearing the workers, the old man thought that perhaps he should get off and walk for a while, which is what he did. Not much further down the road, they passed a group of merchants, who began muttering among themselves, "Isn't it terrible that a healthy young boy is riding while his poor grandfather is walking!" Hearing this, the old man and the boy promptly switched places and continued traveling toward the market. Before long, they passed another group of travelers who derided them, calling out, "Look at that mean old man, riding along on the donkey, making the young boy walk so far!" Hearing that, the man got down. But no sooner had he started walking alongside his grandson when they encountered a group of housewives who began laughing, saying, "Look at that stupid old man and boy. They have a fine donkey, and they're walking when they could be riding!"

So, here we are at the dawning of a whole new culture, surrounded with around-the-clock advice on how to best to ride our donkeys into the future. I really believe that now, more than ever, it is vitally important for each of us to re-learn to trust ourselves. To trust our Inner Compass, our relationship to Source, and our ability to make conscious choices that best fit our individual needs and circumstances.

Remembering the Alamo

My friend Guy told me about an image that was burned into his consciousness when he was a child in the early '60s. It is a photo from *LIFE* (magazine), taken at the moment the topmost section of a crowded grandstand began to collapse.

What struck him most about the image was that while people in the top rows were literally falling to their deaths, their faces twisted in horror, the heads of the occupants the next few rows below them were turned around, eyes wide with surprise. In the next, lower section of rows, faces were just beginning to register that something unusual was happening. Meanwhile, down below, hundreds of people were still watching the entertainment in front of them, laughing, talking and eating, completely unaware of the drama unfolding behind them.

Even though I've never even seen the photograph, this image is burned in my memory, too. In part, that's because it's such a graphic example of how a moment or incident can affect different people in different ways, based on their perceptions. Even now, while writing this, I'm experiencing their experience, simply based on the way Guy related his experience of their experience to me.

I've been thinking about this phenomenon in connection with the ongoing controversy about the Battle of the Alamo, which seems to flare up in San Antonio every spring as our city prepares for Fiesta. This annual ten-day stretch of non-stop city-wide parties and parades is as unique to our local culture as Mardi Gras is to New Orleans. Traditionally celebrated as glorious examples of bravery and heroism in the fight for liberty, many people now argue that Davy Crockett, Jim Bowie and their fellow defenders of the Alamo weren't really brave at all. With increasing frequency, they're being portrayed as cowardly or self-serving. Moreover, it is argued that the Alamo does not represent freedom, but racism, colonialism and oppression. Instead of remembering the Alamo, many Texans would prefer to forget its legacy of violence and militarism.

What I find curious about the Battle of the Alamo is that there appears to be no one definitive version of the story, even though this event took place right here in San Antonio less than two hundred years ago. Numerous newspaper reports and handwritten personal accounts must have been available, and yet there are still so many conflicting stories about what happened. Is it any wonder, then, that there are so many different ideas about the history and meaning of the Crucifixion and Resurrection of Jesus Christ, another controversy often discussed at this time of the year? Most Biblical historians now agree that the New Testament was derived from oral histories recorded by a number of authors, beginning at least ten years after the Crucifixion and continuing for at least 150 years. Various versions were written and compiled in several stages and in several different languages before the canon we've come to know as the Bible was adopted over 300 years after the last eyewitnesses to Jesus' life and death had died.

So what is the "gospel truth" about the Easter story? At one level, that's like asking what the truth is about the Alamo or which of the people in the grandstand knew what was actually happening at the time the *LIFE* photo was taken. Who really knows?

While ongoing scholarship and speculation about the past may be interesting to some, I choose to focus my energy on the present. Personally, I'm not as concerned with who died at the Alamo or why as I am with how I can live to make those deaths meaningful, how I can help heal the scars of our violent history. And as interesting as the details of the death and Resurrection of Jesus might be, for me the more important question is: How can I allow Spirit to become truly alive in my life? The fact that there are no easy answers to such questions doesn't make asking them any less important.

Behind the Velvet Curtain

It is springtime, and the signs and symbols of renewal surround us. Wildflowers, trees, Easter eggs and warm breezes are tapping us on the shoulder, reminding us of the newness all around and within us. Inviting us to remember that we, too, can be renewed, if only we will allow the old to drop away, to be replaced by what wants to blossom inside of us.

Forgiveness can play an integral part in this process of renewal. Yet, all too often all too many of us avoid forgiving ourselves and others because we think that there's something hard we need to do. In fact forgiveness is simply a state of being.

Forgiveness has a sweet, juicy taste, like the ripest of mangoes or freshly picked peaches. It satisfies a deep-down hunger we seem to carry, half-forgotten, stuffed in the dark, dusty corners of our hearts. And it is only when we allow ourselves to be touched by the healing power of forgiveness that we remember just how much we have been hurting in silence. How we have been skirting the small sadnesses accumulated in a lifetime: the bruises our little bodies sustained on the playgrounds of childhood; the scars inflicted by adolescent dating (or the painful lack thereof); unfounded stories told by well-meaning friends and parents; stinging remarks made by passing strangers. Whether all these half-hidden hurts occurred long ago, in yesteryear or just yesterday, they tend to keep bouncing around inside of us, exploding at random intervals, like hand grenades with time-delayed fuses. That is, unless we choose otherwise.

Yes, forgiveness is a choice, one that only you can make. But be aware that your ego will try its best to stop you from making such a choice. That's because forgiveness can seem like certain death to your ego, threatening its livelihood as judge, jury and chief defender of your pride and shame. Not wanting to surrender, it keeps playing its game, over and over, declaring itself winner time and again.

Still, as you willingly take the risk of moving through your discomfort anyway, forgiveness brushes against your cheek like a velvet curtain, immensely soft and certainly comforting. And then, the curtain is magically drawn back to show you previously unseen possibilities singing the joyful chorus that your soul has been longing to hear: "Come home! Come home! Ally-ally-ox-come-free!" they sing out to you.

The real miracle of forgiveness is a gift to the giver as well as the receiver. Both taste the sweetness of the fruit, juice dribbling down their chins. Whether or not a single word has ever been said aloud, or a single physical action has been taken, both giver and receiver are brushed by the velvet curtain, pulled back to show that there is no separation, and never was, except in our hearts and minds.

That brings up a simple question: Who or what can you forgive today? And what in the world are you waiting for?

Shopping for Shoes

I've often been accused of wearing ugly shoes, to which I cheerfully plead guilty as charged. Because I freely admit that I've tended towards clunky-looking, practical shoes ever since my groovy but narrow-toed Beatle boots began hurting my feet when I was a freshman in high school. That's when I decided that any future fashion statements I made would have to come from above my ankles. For a brief period now, my Birkenstocks and Rockports have actually been sort of trendy. But I can already see that fad coming to an end. I don't care. Give me a comfortable, durable, if slightly unfashionable pair of shoes any day.

I've noticed that clerks tend to get a little flustered when I go shoe shopping. That's because if I'm interested in a particular pair of shoes, I really put them through the paces right there in the store. I jump around, walk fast and slow, run, come to screeching halts, try to click my heels in mid-air. If the shoes aren't comfortable enough to run, dance and play in, I don't want to walk in them either! After a minute or two of this activity, the bemused salesperson usually asks, "How do you like them?" And I say, "Well, I haven't had them on long enough to know yet." And I'll just keep moving around the store until I get a clear sense of whether or not I want that particular pair. I have noticed, however, that some of the best shoes don't feel immediately comfortable. It takes a while to break them in and to get used to the very characteristics that make them special. So I really have to listen to my body while I'm in the store, trusting that my feet will tell me whether the discomfort I feel is temporary or a permanent part of the shoe.

Although I wouldn't want to push this analogy too far, I guess I feel much the same way about spirituality. These days, there seems to be a veritable explosion of spiritual "lessons" jumping out at us from workshops, lectures, bookstores, bulletin boards, and television. Even the magazine racks in the grocery stores are packed with advice on "how to live a happier, healthier, more holistic life." How can I know who and/or what to believe? On which path should I focus my time and energy?

Personally, the only thing I'm sure of is that I want a spirituality I can live with day-in, day-out, not just on one day of the week or when I'm with a particular group of people. For me, it's not enough that a particular teaching sounds good coming out of a lecturer's mouth, or makes for a snappy quote from a currently best-selling self-help book. Whenever I come across an appealing notion, I try to remember to ask myself, "Can I really use this? Does it make sense? Can I apply it in relationship with my family and friends? Can I bear witness to Spirit by living this teaching?" If so, I test it, wear it, try it out for a while. If it fits, fine. And if not, I don't argue with it or try to change anybody else's ideas about it. I just leave it for somebody else.

In my work as an artist, workshop leader and minister, I've come into contact with so many different spiritual teachers and teachings. I don't pretend to understand them all, much less agree with them. Nor would I expect to. As far as I can tell, my task is simply to remain as open as possible, to honor all spiritual traditions and their potential for feeding my Soul, without needing to figure out which one or why or how. To be willing to learn from the underlying truths informing all of the great spiritual traditions while remembering that the Buddha once said there are eighty-eight thousand paths to Enlightenment — and that was over two thousand years ago, long before there was a self-help industry spinning out new metaphysical technologies at a mind boggling rate.

I can't try out all those paths, any more than I could or would want to try out every pair of shoes at a shoe store. But when I do find a teaching that seems to fit, it's worth the effort to dig deeper, try it on, spend some time listening to what my body, mind and Spirit all have to say about it. As far as I can tell, comfort and durability are just as important for our Souls as for our soles.

There is no perfect time to meditate.

There is only now.

Walking Gently

My friend David died after a long illness which gave him a lot of time to come to peace with his death. And because he felt fairly comfortable talking about his departure, he told several people to make sure that there be no big funeral. He simply wanted to be cremated, for a few folks to gather in his little house and spread his ashes throughout his beloved rose garden.

When the time came, that's exactly what happened. Except he'd made so many friends through his years as a respected actor, author, publisher and patron of the arts that a somber mob of us ended up standing crowded, shoulder to shoulder, in his living room. We shared memories, recited favorite passages, spoke loving words. We hummed the *Ode to Joy* together, laughed a bit, cried a lot, then took turns shuffling through the patio door to scatter spoonfuls of David's ashes between the roses.

The garden had been freshly turned and enhanced with a variety of colorful bedding plants. A slight breeze chased all the clouds from the bright blue sky, setting a perfect backdrop for bidding farewell to our friend. After we'd scattered the last of his ashes, there wasn't much left to say, so most of us simply left, going our separate ways in silence.

Walking back to my car, I glanced down at my feet and suddenly realized that my shoes were covered with an unfamiliar gray powder. I was wearing David on my shoes, walking on my friend's remains! Feeling somewhat shocked and embarrassed, my first reflex was to wipe them off before anyone else noticed. I bent down and slapped my right shoe briskly, only to discover that (a) the ashes mostly stuck to the leather and (b) the few ashes that had left my shoe were now smeared on my hands. Now what?

Standing there with my friend's ashes clinging to my fingers and feet, I began laughing silently, helplessly into the empty sky. Suddenly a flashing light went off in the back of my brain. Every fiber of my being began pulsating with the startling experience of feeling intimately connected to the ground I was standing on, the air I was breathing. What is soil, after all, but the powdered leftovers of seashells and seashores, treetops and dinosaurs, bird feathers and forefathers? And haven't scientists been telling us that the air on our precious little planet is of a fairly limited quantity, continually recycled from being to being? That every lung full we inhale is almost certain to contain at least a few of the self-same molecules exhaled by a Napoleon, Einstein, Saddam Hussein or a peasant working in China sometime earlier.

Of course, I'd long known these facts intellectually, but this was different. This was a spine-tingling, goose-bumpy, Humpty-Dumpty kind of experience. One which arrived blowing bells and whistles into the far corners of my head and heart simultaneously. My next step was taken very gently, knowing that I was literally carrying David, both in my soul and on my soles. Knowing that sooner or later, my ashes, too, will become fertilizer under someone else's shoes — perhaps yours.

The First Morning in Our New House

After spending the first night in our new house,
I wake up inside the song of a mourning dove
calling, calling, calling my six-year-old eyes to
come see the surprises outside the bedroom window:
a gigantic green lawn, stretching on and on,
fresh white paint on the wooden frame walls,
three hackberry trees so tall
that they demand young hands to
build grand treehouses as soon as possible,
long tangles of mustang grapevines,
loaded with fruit and promises of adventure.

Without turning around, I hear the sounds of
my older brother asleep in the other bed.
My head spins knowing that just the two of us have
this huge room,
two desks,
a big closet and six bookshelves
all to ourselves.

Four younger brothers are sleeping in their own room
in this house that is so much bigger than
our family's dreams have ever been.
I look at my sleepy face in the mirror and ask,
"Is this too good to be true?"

Only thirty years later do the shadows appear
in that same closet, whispering,
"This house has cost your father so much."
Hours spent working overtime, weaving in the textile mill,
nights spent worrying alone in the dark,
years spent regretting not spending more time
playing with his sons while they were still young enough
to care whether he was there
or not.

Only now am I beginning to feel his hunger and hear
the moaning of my childhood shoes
waiting,
waiting,
waiting
to walk and talk and play ball with him.

summer

At the Beach

Surging waves urge young hearts to action
while the Gulf breeze demands some degree of surrender.
Head down, the young beachcomber keeps walking
at the water's edge searching
for something his eyes haven't seen before.

"Don't go out into the deep water," warns my father.
"You can't see the undertow, but it's there,
it's dangerous,
it will suck you under
and I won't be able to save you."

The man is eager for a little quiet fishing time on his own
during this rare family outing at the beach.
Knowing it is his job to keep watch over his excited sons,
he casts a nervous eye on six young pairs of arms and legs
scattered across the shoreline,
all straining to find the beat
inside the freedom song of the surf.

I am a good boy, and easily scared as well.
To this day, I seldom let myself go out deeper
where the big waves dance and call my name.

Shelter from the Swelter

Like many folks who grew up in this area, I've gotten pretty used to living in air-conditioned comfort during the hot, sticky South Texas summer days. I'm very grateful that we have AC these days, and would definitely miss it if it were to disappear. But I've also become increasingly aware of how much it costs and how much we've lost by closing our windows and doors to the sweltering heat. In the process, we not only close ourselves off from the warmth, but from our environment and from each other as well. I suppose living in our Victorian cottage in the King William neighborhood has made me particularly sensitive to this subject. Most of the houses in this area were built long ago, with the high ceilings, tall windows, front porches, and screen doors that made cross-ventilation possible and life tolerable in the days before AC. I think there's something magical about opening those windows during a rainfall or after nightfall, when the cooling breezes come blowing in from the Southeast; something musical about waking up to the sounds of birds stirring in the pre-dawn stillness; something special about sitting in the front porch swing, drinking a slow cup of tea and greeting neighbors out for their early morning walks in the unique coolness that only a summer sunrise brings.

And, yes, I know that many people would disagree, in part because most folks now live in houses and apartments that simply weren't built to allow for such ventilation, even if they so desired. Still I can't help wanting to urge others to share in the particular pleasures that the summer brings to those who linger outside in the early mornings and late evenings. If that's already part of your lifestyle, you know what I mean. And if not, consider taking a little time sometime this month to go outside, whether early or late, and simply sit doing nothing for a little while. It's in this spirit that I offer this poem:

Wrapped in a robe of sunlit silence,
the armless red rocking chair takes me back
to where I haven't been for far too long,
moving in place, back and forth,
noiseless as the swishing of my tabby cat's tail.
Just five minutes earlier,
I was firmly wrapped in a relentless hurry –
barely past sunrise and already my plate was full
of projects, plans and unkept promises,
feeling sullen and surly,
wondering how did it get so late so early?

This quiet moment
snuck over the threshold on soft-slippered feet
first catching me by surprise,
now holding me as willing captive.
This is my Waterloo,
and I surrender to you, little rocking chair.
Feed your prisoner steamed brown rice, one grain at a time.
Water my thirsty heart, tear my well-planned day apart.

Alone Together

The rains finally came to San Antonio! After a record heat spell and prolonged drought, the rains and cool(er) temperatures are a blessing. Of course, as is often the case, the change in weather was a mixed blessing, as fierce winds and hail accompanied the storm when it first blew in. We're fortunate it wasn't as disastrous as elsewhere in South Texas, but it was certainly bad enough.

In our historic neighborhood of King William, south of downtown, the damage was significant. The brick chimney on one neighbor's two-story Victorian house toppled over. Another neighbor was startled to hear a giant, Red Oak tree come crashing down in her yard. Its forty-eight inch trunk remained intact, but its roots pulled free from gravity's hold. Many more stately trees lost huge limbs, and all of our gardens were pelted and littered with leaves and small branches.

On Saturday morning, after two full days of hard winds and rain, the clouds parted and the sun came out with a vengeance. As if on cue, up and down the block neighbors popped out of houses carrying rakes, saws, brooms and ladders. We all set to the task of cleaning up after the storm, clearing gutters, sweeping walkways, trimming limbs and stacking branches for trash pickup.

The work felt good, reminding me that while exercising for the sake of exercise can be fun, it feels even better to work up a sweat doing the kind of physical labor that produces tangible results. In this instance, what made the work especially enjoyable was the spontaneous camaraderie among our neighbors.

We live in a friendly neighborhood anyway, one where most of us know each other well enough to call out names in passing, or at least wave hello and make small talk periodically. But on this occasion, something magical occurred. Almost all of us started out working separately, tending to our own turf, but ended up working together, supporting each other, loaning tools, holding ladders, lugging limbs. Some just gave moral support, stopping to comment and commiserate or to make jokes from across the driveway. Connected by close proximity and the common job at hand, we worked individually, but together. By mid-afternoon it was over. With our houses and yards in order once more, we all went back indoors to our semi-secret lives.

But the energy of the experience remains. Among other things, it strikes me as a metaphor for one of the most important things we can do in a lifetime: building community, making vital connections at the personal, social and spiritual levels. When the storms strike or when the good times roll, it helps to have a community to share the experiences with. Of course, we still have to do the work ourselves, but it sure feels better knowing we're not alone in the process. As my friend Charly likes to say, "You have to do it by yourself, but you can't do it alone."

Deep in the Canyon

This is an excerpt from a letter I wrote to Zet during the course of a mind-boggling, heart-opening, life-changing two-week rafting trip through the Grand Canyon.

"Someone maintains that today is Sunday; it takes the rest of us by surprise because we've lost track of time and the days of the week. What we focus on instead are the rhythms of the sun rising and setting, the cycles of rapids and smooth water...

"Since it is Sunday, I lead a morning meditation and sing and read a poem as sunrise peeks over the rim. Daybreak here is at about 5:00 a.m., and even the hardcore night owls in our group are getting used to being up and around and cheerful — or at least congenial — by 5:15. An amazing process to watch. Of course, we quickly fall asleep after sundown. Campfires aren't allowed in the Canyon and the work/heat/excitement of the day have even the hardiest party-ers in their sleeping bags by 9:30 p.m., at the latest.

"Almost every night, however, the stars wake me up with their midnight brightness and majesty, leaving me awake with sheer awe and wonder. There is something jarring about lying at the bottom of this huge deep hole in the earth, with its black walls looming massively overhead, framing a slice of silently thundering galaxies, shooting stars and moonbeams staring at me, commanding me to watch a dance of infinite depth and snail-paced grace unfolding.

"Later, floating quietly down the river in a long stretch between rapids, I could swear I felt the folks in the Celebration Circle back home beginning the service with an invocation. A rush of connectedness and well-being came over me and called me into a communion of spirits. Checking a guide's watch, I confirmed that it was shortly after 11:00 in your time zone. As I began to pray with you, I found myself caught in a mind trap, trying to visualize you and our friends, trying to hear you and how the music sounded. Trying to be there, instead of simply being here. But after awhile I literally came to my senses and opened my eyes and heart to where I was, in this magnificent natural cathedral. I took it in as fully as possible, then did my best to transmit to everyone in the Circle the peacefulness and splendor, the song of creation unfolding, the miracle of spontaneous worship…

"And that is what I am doing now, too. The rest of the group is off on a hike up the Little Colorado. I stopped part-way and am sitting in the shade, somewhat protected from the 105° heat. Feeling grace and gratitude, sending my love with a happy heart and an opening mind. My main hope is to carry this awareness back home to the Circle and all the circles of my life."

What I focus on expands.

What do I choose to focus on?

Silence in the Desert

It happened years ago, but I can still hear it as if it had been last week. Zet and I were driving through Arizona on our way to work at a seminar in California. As has often been the case on such working road trips, we were in a hurry, traveling long hours in order to get from one job to the next on time. Feeling tired and bored with the monotony of driving on the interstate highway, I took a detour onto a smaller road, which led us into the heart of the desert.

After driving on that road awhile, the scenery became increasingly magnificent, urging me to pull over, get out and risk the searing heat. Leaving my air-conditioned womb, I wandered out into the bright, hot landscape. I walked aimlessly for a little while, struck by the majesty of this wide-open bigness, stretching out for miles and miles in all directions. Perhaps most striking of all was the silence. At first the lack of sound seemed eerie, almost deafening. But as I stood still, awestruck by the immediacy of my surroundings, I began hearing a whole host of small sounds: the intermittent scratching of two lizards darting between the sage bushes; the whirring of a grasshopper; the distinct descending notes of a canyon wren, off in the distance. It took a while longer to hear the chorus of quiet pops and cracks all around me — and longer still before I could identify them as being the voices of the many rocks lying on the ground, expanding with the rising temperatures of the late morning sun. At least, that was what my mind hypothesized as a way of making sense of the fact that the rocks surrounding me were literally singing out loud!

Then from far off came a strange, high-pitched whine. Gradually it grew lower and louder until it became the familiar roar of a pickup truck speeding by, then trailing off into the distance for what seemed like an extraordinarily long time. I was stunned to find myself so strongly affected by the sound of one lone truck driving by. Resenting the noisy intrusion, my mind leapt into overdrive, trying to calculate and comprehend how much noise pollution is generated in the daily lives of city dwellers like myself, surrounded by countless cars, machines, etc. From there it was just a small step into righteous indignation over the many costs of our modern lifestyle, mixed with equal parts rage, regret and romantic notions of how peaceful it would be to live in such a desert setting.

Smack dab in the middle of this flight of fantasy, I became aware of the loudest noise of all: the sound of my mind interpreting sensations, making judgments, spinning stories out of thin air. Suddenly, swiftly, all too briefly, I slipped into a state of absolute inner silence, spellbound by the beauty and peace that exists in the space between my thoughts. It was indescribably delicious and infinitely restful.

But all too soon my mind kicked back into gear with a thud, loudly inserting its evaluation of the experience I'd just had. Informing me of my obligations, reminding me that we had miles to go before we could sleep. Surrendering with a sigh, I walked back to the car, rested, refreshed and ready for the remainder of the journey.

I don't know how long I'd been standing in that shimmering sandscape, probably less than half an hour. And really, nothing had happened. Yet, the experience has stayed with me for years, serving as a beacon to that place of inner peace and silence. Periodically, it invites me to take a few minutes to simply stop in my tracks and tune in to my surroundings, listening to the ever more subtle sounds until I encounter the silence in the space between my thoughts. It takes a little practice, but it doesn't take much skill. I'm pretty sure that almost anyone can do it. It just begins with a willingness to pause and listen. How about right now?

Walking in the Dark

Our son, Mateo, just turned two. An exciting age. Young enough that his world is still a brand new book, each page an adventure. Old enough to begin making connections, humming with the excitement of discovering patterns in the sights and sounds surrounding him. It's been particularly delicious watching him explore the fields, trees and treasures in and around our new house. So much to see, so much energy; so little timidity. His drive toward independence is as visible and delightful as his extravagantly thick, wavy mop of hair. Granted, that same independence can be mighty inconvenient for his parents, to say nothing of being downright infuriating at times. But by and large I stay in awe of the way his little legs carry him forward with a confidence I can only dream of acquiring.

We go for walks almost daily. I usually find myself following in his footsteps, just far enough behind to let him lead the way, just close enough to protect him from danger. Most of the time his eyes remain focused on the trail ahead, but every once in awhile, something will perplex him, some noise will scare him and he'll scurry back in my direction. Or, seeking safety and affirmation in the face of danger, he'll simply turn to me and scream, "Papa, Papa!" Then, after a hug or two and a few moments of reassurance, he zooms off again in search of new discoveries.

It seems to me that in times of trouble, many adults (myself included) tend to act a lot like Mateo. Full of ourselves, we truck along pretending that we're free agents, independent of everybody else — as long as things are going well. It is only when we come face to face with uncertainty or danger, whether real or imagined, that our impulse is to turn around and look for help, hoping for someone to come to our rescue. Sort of like the story about the six-year old who was scared of the dark. One night, right before bedtime, his mother noticed that he'd left his bicycle outside in the front yard. When she told him to go put it in the garage, he protested that it was too dark outside. She reminded him that there was nothing to be scared of, and besides, God would protect him. Somewhat mollified, but not convinced, he stuck his head out the front door and yelled, "God, are you out there?" Not hearing any answer, he ducked back inside and tried to dissuade his mother once again. But she would not be moved, and merely reminded him that it was past his bedtime. Reluctantly, the boy went back to the door, and yelled again, "God, are you out there?" Still no answer. "Well, if you're out there, please put my bicycle in the garage for me!"

We hope that some other person, some organization, some Higher Power — in short, "Anybody-else-but-me" will take care of the perceived threat. And at those times when "the rescuer" is not immediately forthcoming, many of us have a tendency to turn to drugs, overeating, shopping or other addictive behaviors to relieve our tension. Sooner or later, however, we begin to tire of the emotional rollercoaster. We set out to find another path, another way of walking through the darkness. And as we continue to mature emotionally and spiritually, the forces of life conspire to teach us that there are other options for dealing with our fears, that it's an inside job. We begin to learn that whatever the appearances, whatever the circumstances, we always have the resources we need to deal with the challenge at hand, if only we can still our monkey minds long enough to remember this is so. To connect with the in–dwelling presence of God, where an infinite supply of love, wisdom, wealth and resources are available to us. We learn we still have to do our part, but that we are never alone.

It's a hard lesson to learn and an easy one to forget, because it's contrary to most of what our ego-centered, action-oriented, dominant culture teaches us about ourselves. However, I believe that with compassion, patience, and practice, we can move beyond our knee-jerk reactions to fear and learn new ways to respond with love and courage instead. In doing so, we are writing an important new story about who we are and who we are becoming. As philosopher Jean Houston says, "Change the story, and you change perception. Change perception, and you change the world."

Not that I've mastered the process by any means. I freely admit that I still forget from time to time and find myself feeling fearful while walking in the dark. But I'm committed to remembering the truth, and I have made it a point to associate with other folks who have made the same commitment, too. We remind each other, again and again that We are One with our deepest selves, each other and the Holy One reflected in all of creation. And I truly believe that as we continue to practice this awareness together, we'll stumble our way toward Paradise, only to discover that's where we've been living all along! That's my story, and I'm sticking to it.

All Day Long

All day long the boy bounces
from one pocket of pleasure to the next.
His second birthday still lives way off
in a distant future that doesn't interest him in the least.
He's far too busy being right here,
moving freely through his days and nights,
answering unheard questions.

His flights of fancy, unencumbered by the weight of words,
find their own way of making sense.
Picking up a piece of lint from under the sofa,
he squeals his delight of discovery,
holds the fluff up to the light, lets go
and watches it drift downward in a long, lazy spiral.
Like him, it is in no hurry either.

He stands on tiptoes,
grabs a bottle of vitamins from the table,
shakes it again and again, rattling the pills,
dancing to a rhythm only he can hear.

He runs through the backyard, barefoot again,
screeches to a halt to pick up a shiny rock.
Feeling its particular weight and contours,
he sticks it in his mouth
and smiles at his invisible cohorts.

A Modest Vacation

Would you like to take a mini–vacation soon? To go on an exotic, fascinating trip? One that is almost certain to dazzle your senses, give you startling new insights into life, and won't cost you a penny?

Here's how: Take a vow of silence for a day, maybe two. A longer period is wonderful if you can manage it, but a shorter one works too, if that's all you can handle. Regardless of the amount of time involved, all this "vacation" (derived from the Latin word *vacatio*, meaning freedom) requires is freeing yourself from talking out loud. That means making a commitment to not speak (except in emergencies, of course) while still going about the business of your daily life. You'll be amazed at how it changes the way the world looks and sounds. I was amazed and amused when I tried this for two days.

It wasn't really planned. It just happened that one day I was feeling overwhelmed by all the writing, phone calls, and appointments I had booked for myself yet again. Feeling fed up and not knowing what else to do, I decided to just stop talking for a while to see what would happen.

Over the years, there have been several times when I was "in the silence" within the context of spiritual retreat settings. But this was different. It involved everyday activities, including a dental appointment, trips to the store, jury duty and household chores. The only physical change I made was to carry a pen and note pad that said: "I can't speak for a few days, but can communicate on paper if you'd like."

Frankly, I was surprised at how seldom I needed to use my pen and paper. I found that people tended to be so preoccupied with their own lives and with what they had to say that few noticed my silence. And I was stunned to discover the sheer volume and variety of background noises surrounding my "normal" life. Experienced at meditation, I thought I was in touch with this noise level. But two short days of refraining from making noise myself revealed layers of sound I never knew existed. Traffic noise was constant. The refrigerator was screaming. The grocery store music was piercing. The humming background sound of conversations in the dentist's office became distinct layers of eavesdropped stories peopled with heroes, villains and plot lines as twisted as any top-rated televised soap opera.

It was also fascinating to note just how pervasive words are. Even when I wasn't talking, so many words entered my head. Things I read, wrote, heard on the radio, said to myself, all ran together in a virtually non-stop conversation. And while that's not necessarily a bad thing, it quickly became clear after just a few hours of silent observation that most of the information passing through my head had nothing to do with what I really want to focus on, like inner peace, purpose, prosperity and the people I love.

Perhaps you're asking, "So what's your point, Rudi?" Well, I could write more about how beautiful the world looked and how peaceful it felt with the sound turned down, even in the middle of a crowded store. I could describe how delicious food tasted in the silence of a meal without words or what a jewel a few minutes of focused prayer became in the setting of a day of silence. But, rather than describe more of my experience, I invite you to enjoy your own experience in the heart of silence. Take a front row seat as a silent spectator in the theater of your own life, and observe yourself playing a non-speaking role for a change.

A caveat: As with any other vacation, there is the risk that you may find this trip into silence either restful or restless. But, whether you find yourself comforted or uncomfortable, chuckling or challenged, I can guarantee that you'll experience enough of a change to make your investment of time and energy more than worthwhile.

Swinging Along

Zet and I went to a carnival with our nieces and nephews recently. They wanted to ride all the rides, especially those stomach-churners that I wouldn't enter on a $1,000 bet. So I spent a good part of the afternoon sitting around in the shade, waiting for the kids and engaging in one of my favorite activities: people watching. I had a particularly interesting time observing the folks at the bell-ringing game. You know, the one where the contestant swings a huge sledgehammer, striking a lever which sends a weighted ball zooming up a pole toward a bell. It's an amazingly primitive form of entertainment, but very engaging. A crowd would always gather to cheer and jeer each person brave enough to pay $2 and try his hand at it. I say "his" because with just one exception, only guys tried it. They varied from teenagers to middle-agers, but they were mostly big, beefy-looking guys. And the bigger the contestant, the more people would gather around to watch, hoping to see someone win the prize.

I was surprised to see that the size of a contestant's muscles had a relatively low correlation to how high the ball went. As a matter of fact, the only person who actually managed to ring the bell during the time we were watching was a relatively slender, though obviously athletic young man. I was puzzled about this until Zet pointed out that he had swung the sledgehammer with focused force, rather than brute force. Sure enough, as I watched other more muscle-bound guys try it, I saw them swinging hard but without much control of the hammer. Consequently, they tended to have a hitch in their swing and/or hit the lever off center. The smaller man spent some time slowly swaying the hammer back and forth, building momentum with his rhythmic swing. Then, at just the right moment, he let the hammer do the work of going around in a slow, steady full circle and landing dead center on the lever. Bingo!

It wasn't exactly an earth-shattering revelation. Just another interesting reminder of something I already knew, but forget all too often: A small amount of focused energy is usually more effective than a larger amount of scattered energy. Just think about it. How often have you (and I) expended a lot of effort trying to make something happen, only to have it fizzle out? Or conversely, isn't it wonderful when you remember to take your time before beginning a physically or emotionally challenging task, getting focused and aligned with your Life Force before taking action?

No doubt I'll encounter other ways to apply this lesson to my everyday life as I ease my way through the summer. Maybe you will, too.

The Moon and Her Sister

There we were. Looking up into the night sky, remembering our sweet friend, Cascade, who had died two days earlier, on the morning of the June Full Moon. It figures. In her final exit, as with so many of her entrances, Cas had a soft, easy touch and an excellent sense of timing. I wouldn't see her for months, even years, at a time. And then, there would be those twinkling eyes smiling at me from the middle of some grocery store aisle or just there on a city sidewalk. But whatever the location, she would invariably appear in the middle of an otherwise difficult day — just when I really needed the joy and encouragement she always seemed to carry with her.

Now that Cas was gone, a bunch of her friends and family members were hanging around the house with her husband Dave. He was trying hard to be brave, and we were all trying equally hard to be helpful and hopeful in the face of her seemingly senseless death from cancer. Normally we would have stayed inside their cool house on such a hot summer night. It's a beautiful home, one they had been building by hand for several years on a 10-acre parcel of land they'd cleared in the Texas Hill Country.

But it was clearly a night to be outdoors honoring our dead sister's deep love for Mother Earth. So we strolled outside, leaving the house in ones and twos, taking the path out to where her ashes will be scattered later, in her favorite oak grove, a couple of hundred yards from the house. As we walked, the last drops of daylight soaked through the branches of the Spanish Oaks and cedar trees overhead. When we got to the grove, we tried to light the large Mexican candle someone had placed in the middle of a circle of stones. But it wouldn't stay lit; the breezes came too strong and too often to let the flame live.

That didn't stop us from drumming, chanting, listening to the sound of the sun sinking into the horizon, watching the light reflect from each other's eyes in the gathering darkness. Someone had brought a flute, someone else two Brazilian rainsticks and a guitar. Only one person had a handkerchief, but nobody needed it. For during the time we sat in that circle together, we were strong and brave, connected as we were by the total mystery of such an unkind death. The questions were mostly unspoken, lurking in the backs of our heads: *Why Cas? Why one so classy, so young, so strong for so long? Why would Death want to come claim someone so vibrant, so talented, with a teenage daughter and a husband who loved her so deeply?*

The Big Questions don't really seem to go away or get solved by addressing them to God/dess. But it does seem that engaging in sacred rituals can help us mortals find some measure of peace in the presence of the great mysteries, can help us remember that there is much more to the histories of our lives than what we can measure with our eyes, account for with our spreadsheets, organize within the boundaries of our appointment books. Shared rituals seem especially helpful when a difficult life passage needs to be maneuvered by folks who would otherwise feel ill-equipped to handle their thoughts and feelings.

So there we were. A score of middle-aging Flower Children and several of our teenaged charges — singing, talking, listening, praying and swaying for a surprisingly short hour. Then suddenly, Jane, one of Cascade's best friends, spotted the Moon making her grand entrance above a nearby pasture. One by one, we stopped singing and drumming and drifted over to where Jane stood transfixed. By the time we'd all gotten to the clearing, even the youngest of the children was quiet. Everyone had run out of words. The only thing that made sense was to stand there in total silence, facing the moon, asking our questions, feeling the evening breezes, embracing each other and our memories of Cascade.

One of our chantsongs from earlier in the evening had travelled a quarter of a million miles, echoed off the face of the moon and came back to reflect in my inner ear:

"Sister is gone, but She's still here.
Sister is gone but She's still here.
The wind is blowing through our tears.
Sister is gone, but She's still here.

Sister is gone, but the Moon still rise.
Sister is gone, but the Moon still rise.
Sister's shining through our eyes.
Sister is gone, but the Moon still rise..."

Painting the Porch

It's been quite a busy summer at our house. Among other things, we had the opportunity to re-do the front porch of our Victorian cottage. We were fortunate to receive a generous restoration grant from the San Antonio Conservation Society. The grant paid for all the supplies and contractors, but did not include the painting. So Zet and I have been prepping and painting the detailed woodwork off and on for a couple of weeks now.

We've done a fair amount of this kind of work over the years, so we sort of knew what we were getting into. But we hadn't counted on having one of the hottest Junes in history. Combined with my awareness of all the other projects and deadlines bearing down on our overheated desktops, the oppressive heat made me feel tired and very put upon as I was painting in the yard.

Then one morning, I got tired of working so hard and decided that the easiest solution was to make a game of it, to go ahead and do the work, but from a different perspective. The rules were simple: Pretend this painting project was really a Creative Living class I'd signed up and paid for. My homework assignment for the week was to note the number of spiritual lessons being presented. Here are some of the things I learned in class:

1. **Slow down and relax.** The work gets done a lot faster when I'm working slower. Trying to paint things in a hurry just means I'll spend more time cleaning up mistakes later.

2. Focus on the little things. Paint one small area at a time. It's helpful to check in and take a look at the Big Picture, the larger task, periodically but not too often. The real work is done one small patch at a time.

3. More is not always better. It's tempting to load the brush with paint, because it seems to go faster. But the more paint on the brush, the harder it is to control; the less paint, the more control and fewer mistakes.

4. Work is more pleasant in the company of friends. It's not only more fun, but much easier painting alongside someone else. There's just more energy available wherever two or more are gathered and focused on the work at hand. Even when Zet was painting on the other side of the house, I swear I could feel the energy of working together — or feel the drop in energy when she went off to take care of some unrelated business.

5. Remember to breathe consciously, especially when faced with a particularly tricky task. It makes a big difference in a quiet little way.

So, that's what I've learned so far. Both the front porch and the Creative Living class are definitely still works in progress. But that's the joy of owning an old house and of being enrolled as a perpetual student in the School of Life. I just hope the next class session is held in a cooler classroom.

Virgil's Latin Class

As a professional writer, performance artist and spiritual director, I love the fact that my work takes a variety of forms. But from time to time, I feel the dark shadow of fear fall over my heart. A sense of inadequacy takes hold, a feeling that I don't really know what my "job" is, much less whether I'm "doing it right" anymore. At times like that I try to remember the story that my late father-in-law, Virgil, told me shortly after Zet and I began our work with the Celebration Circle. When I confessed to feeling unprepared for the position I'd taken, he pulled me aside and told me about his first teaching job.

Having been a Little All-American football star at Kansas Wesleyan College, he'd readily found a position as a high-school coach upon graduation, just as he'd hoped. But when he reported to Inman High School the week before school started, the principal informed him that the Latin teacher had abruptly resigned for health reasons and that Virgil would have to teach a Latin class in addition to his other duties. When Virgil protested that he wasn't qualified to teach Latin, the principal explained that there wasn't any choice if he still wanted the job as coach. So Virgil did the only thing he knew to do. He took the Latin textbook home and crammed all week. On the first day of school, he introduced himself to his new students, saying, "Hello, I'm Coach Baer, your Latin teacher. To tell you the truth, I don't know much

Latin, but I've been studying this textbook pretty hard. I'm on page fifty. Catch me if you can!" And, throughout that school year, none of his students did!

Something about the spirit of that story rests my soul. It reminds me that whatever my fears might try to tell me, my commitment and willingness to serve is enough. I don't need to measure up to some self-created yardstick. I certainly don't claim to be fifty pages ahead of anyone, by any means. But I also know that I'm not behind anyone else either. I've simply decided to walk alongside those who choose to walk the path of conscious co-creation. Everything else about this work is a mystery. And for now, that's just fine with me.

The Day before the Autum Equinox

Sweating…
The newspaper says a cold front is due
on Monday night or Tuesday.
Soon the heat and humidity will be a memory.
Sweaters and corduroys will take the place of
T-shirts and shorts.

But for now,
my yellow Labrador puppy lies panting on the floor.
I promise her a cool respite,
but she doesn't even raise her head.
I don't believe me either.

A sticky warm blanket of hopelessness hangs heavy
on my desktop where only the growing pile of past-due bills
and unanswered phone call notes
seem to have any chance of wresting desk space
from the ever creeping, growing grayness.

The front door blows open briefly.
A breeze comes sneaking through the room
sending papers flying,
neutralizing the sweat on my face
just for a moment or two,
brushing my hair softly with a touch of sweet relief.

The puppy stands and wags her tail
to greet this welcome visitor.

autumn

Another Summer Died

A cold north wind whips into town, stealing warmth
and banishing half-empty bottles of suntan lotion
to the back shelf of the bathroom closet.

Another deadline dribbles by
and slides off into the growing shadows.
Another Halloween night sinks out of sight,
playing more tricks than treats, by far too large a margin.
Another box of woolen sweaters pulled out of storage,
full of moth holes, unfit to wear in public places.

The first chilly morning of the year
dares bare toes to go ahead:
leave the comfort of your bed,
touch the freezing floorboards
with feet grown unaccustomed to this temperature.

Another bowl of steaming oatmeal turns cold and slimy
in the time between the stovetop and the table.
Another summer died while you weren't looking,
or were busy cooking up plans for a next year
in which you were going to live without fear or failure.

Meanwhile, the cold north wind whips into town,
stealing warmth and banishing unopened dreams of bigness
back into the closet
and whispers from beneath your pillow:
Don't wait.   Don't wait.   Don't wait.

Putting the Heart before the Horse

As another election year rolls into high gear there is a distinct ugliness in the air. It is not restricted to any one candidate or political party. Even the "alternative" voices are sending out shrill–sounding appeals based on what I consider false economic assumptions: that there is not enough to go around and that someone or something "out there" is taking our share and is somehow to blame for our troubles. Whether the finger is being pointed at tax rates or illegal immigrants, budget deficits or welfare recipients, druglords or corporate CEO's, campaign finance reform or trade agreements — the assumption is that once "They" or "That" is defeated, "Our" well-being will be restored.

Seen from a metaphysical perspective, this reasoning is backwards. It is a matter of putting the proverbial cart before the horse. What we need is to put the heart before both, locate a deep sense of well–being within ourselves as individuals, and then find ways to foster that same feeling within our immediate families and communities.

And therein lies the problem. We live in a society that still pays lip service to the importance of family and community but places little actual value on them. (I won't take the space to argue the point here. If you want to take look at a mind-boggling examination of our society's economic values and assumptions, check out Charles Reich's twenty-fifth anniversary edition of *The Greening of America.* Scary!) While there are as many possible solutions as there are souls on the planet, I believe two of the most forceful and feasible actions we can take as caring individuals are 1) to practice feeling our Oneness with all life on a regular basis and 2) to consciously cultivate community in our personal spheres of influence.

It's exciting to know that the work of the Celebration Circle is part of a burgeoning, world–wide movement of individuals and organizations actively seeking to co-create new ways of being engaged with the planet and each other. In the first place, we are finding ways to expand awareness of our Oneness with all life, while honoring the fact that each person is traveling a unique path. In the second place, we're consciously cultivating a deeper, wider sense of community in our midst.

However, it's not just a matter of patting ourselves on the back and saying, "How nice!" or, to quote the infamous *Saturday Night Live* Church Lady, "Isn't THAT special!" Instead, it is a reminder that what we are doing and creating within the Circle really matters. In a society where so many people feel powerless, disconnected, alienated and depressed, we are reaching out to each other and making a difference — one hug, one dinner date, one conversation, one purchase at a time.

This is the nitty-gritty of that "paradigm shift" and the "New Physics" we keep reading and hearing about in metaphysical books, seminars and talk shows. This is the question we each have to deal with: Can you and I move beyond the false economic assumptions of the Dominator Culture and find ways to re-discover and reinforce our connections to ourselves and each other? When we meet on the street or have a dinner date, can we dare to speak, not just about the weather or sports or food, but also our true feelings? Can we find more ways to be in authentic relationships with people and situations that make us uncomfortable: co–workers, family members, homeless strangers and unseen beings in Bosnia, Mexico and San Antonio? Can we create new patterns of consumption that are environmentally and socially sustainable?

That's a tall order. But who else will do it, if not you and I? And how long can we afford to put it off, in a society where we keep locking more and more doors and feeling less and less secure, even while sending record numbers of our fellow citizens to jail — to say nothing of executing shamefully large numbers of women and men? How many of our churches, graveyards and schools have to get trashed and burglarized? How many of our own children are we going to lock up in prisons and detox centers? How many more soldiers will murder each other before we fathers and mothers rise up and say, "Enough is enough!"

Yes, we need to make our voices heard at the ballot box, too. But we have a lot of groundwork to do before our electoral process can mirror anything but divisiveness back to us anytime in the foreseeable future.

Another Joke on Me

Whatever else may or may not be true about God, I'm sure that S/he has a droll sense of humor. I was reminded of this once again when Zet and I went to Mexico to officiate a wedding for two dear friends who are natives of Mexico City. It was a wonderful occasion, and we were warmly received in the homes of their friends and families. This enabled us to experience a local's view of many of the wonders of Mexico's ancient and varied culture, as well as a moving trip to the Pyramids of Teotihuacan and a romantic stay in Taxco during a total eclipse of the full moon.

For me, the most amazing experience I encountered on that trip had nothing to do with ancient ruins or magnificent meals. It occurred late at night, about a week after arriving, when I awoke with a terrible case of "tourista" or "Traveler's Disease." There I was, all alone, gripped by the worst cramping and nausea imaginable, on my knees in a dark, unfamiliar bathroom, feeling utterly miserable.

In the middle of this gut-wrenching nightmare-come-true, I felt a wave of well-being, love and inner light pass through my whole body. A deep feeling of inner peace and contentment came over me as a voice sounded clearly, saying, "All is well." And strangely enough, I had the instantaneous awareness that all was well, even as I continued vomiting. A few moments later, Zet came in to lay gentle hands and a cool washcloth on the back of my neck, and the whole episode passed into history.

Lying in bed the next day, I had to chuckle at the joke Spirit had played on me. I've spent countless hours of my life in prayer and meditation perched in front of carefully constructed altars. I've participated in a wide range of spiritual studies, support groups, retreats and pilgrimages to faraway Power Spots to connect with the still small voice, only to get this most direct communication while ignominiously hugging a commode in Mexico!

Wrapped inside the joke was a serious reminder to keep my eyes, ears and heart open at all times and places for dancing lessons from God. Let go of expectations of how the spiritual path is "supposed" to unfold. Stay present to the miracles of the Sacred unfolding in the seemingly unimportant, even painful, moments of the mundane. Who knows when and where the next teacher will appear?

Harvest Time

A journalist went to interview Albert Einstein at the height of his fame. Upon entering Einstein's study, the visitor noticed a horseshoe hanging over the door and asked, "You don't actually believe that old superstition about horseshoes bringing good luck, do you?" "Of course not," answered the famous physicist. "Then why do you have that horseshoe hanging there?" prodded the journalist. "Because," replied Einstein with a straight face, "it works whether you believe it or not!"

This anecdote is a gentle reminder that each of us is free to choose what we believe, limited only by the extent to which we are conscious of what we believe in the first place. That's why many of us walking a spiritual path are invited to become increasingly aware of our belief systems and the fruits they bear in our lives. As we consciously examine our old beliefs (most of which we unquestioningly accepted as "The Truth" when we learned them from our parents and peers), and align them more fully with our new understanding of Spirit, amazing things happen in our lives.

This has been demonstrated repeatedly in my life, and most recently in the days leading up to Celebration Circle's first annual silent auction and fun(d)raiser. As the event drew closer, it became obvious that it was going to be extremely successful, as evidenced by the sheer number of donations, inquiries and phone calls flooding our office. It was exhilarating and exhausting, to be in the middle of this swirling whirlwind of energy.

Three days prior to the big day, a good friend asked me how things were going. I replied that it was a rich and wonderful time of harvesting the "crops" we'd been carefully cultivating in the Celebration Circle. "However," I moaned, "this harvest is also a hectic and exhausting time of working long hours to deal with the abundance of support coming in."

I was floored when she answered, "Maybe that's because you're still thinking of the patriarchal model of farming and harvesting one big crop at a time. Perhaps you could entertain a more matriarchal view, one that assumes that Mother Earth is always fertile and supplying all your needs. That means you can harvest continually and ease-fully as you go, because there's no rush and no one big harvest day when all the crops must be harvested at once."

Click! From that point on, I made a conscious choice to view the fun(d)raiser and its attendant details in that light, and it really made a big difference in my experience. There was still a lot of work to do, but at least some of it got done from a consciousness of ease, well being and timelessness. As it turned out, the event was a huge success and far exceeded our goals. And while I am glad for all the gifts given and received during that process, I'm particularly grateful for the opportunity to rethink the nature of harvesting. It was a special gift that will keep on giving for years to come.

The First Cold Front Blew In Last Night

Taste the fullness of the wind
as autumn leaves crunch underfoot
and flocks of swallows flow overhead
from north to south in fitful bursts.
Let your eyes rush out to greet the sky
which grew much taller overnight,
swept clean and turned a brilliant blue
by fall's first chilly blast.

A Red-tailed Hawk cries out to you:
Wake up and watch another turning of the wheel,
another time of dying has come to pay a call.

Stand tall among the falling leaves,
walk fast and hard against the wind
sing wordlessly out loud
and let your singing fill the air
with wonder, joy and gratitude
and sorrow, too, and sense of loss
for all that was and won't return.

Somewhere beyond your line of sight
autumn leaves are being burned
their sweet smoke catches your attention
and takes you for a lonely ride
down long, echoing halls of memories.

You'd like to linger longer, but the chilly wind
demands your attention again and again.
Watch your breath make clouds of steam
watch your mind make up layers of stories
watch the wind making trees release their leaves
reminding you that this is the season
to let go of whatever no longer serves you
or anyone else you can think of.

Just a Minute

The phone had been ringing off the hook for days as a variety of volunteers, vendors and ticket buyers called to verify information regarding the Circle's third annual fundraising event. By coincidence (if there is such a thing), Zet and I were also in the middle of selling our home, while simultaneously negotiating a contract to buy another house. This required multiple meetings, faxes and phone calls with the bankers, buyers, mortgage brokers and owners involved. Meanwhile, our seventeen-month-old son, Mateo, sensing the energy surging all around him, responded by cranking up his speed and volume levels commensurably.

Zet generally wound up taking care of most of the details and phone calls, while I took care of Mateo, ran errands and attempted to do some writing in between times. She is very good at multi-tasking, but I'm not. I felt increasingly frustrated with the activity level in our household. The memory of one particular moment sticks in my mind. Zet was off at yet another meeting, the phone was ringing once again, I was holding a squirming, crying baby on my hip, while stirring the lentils which were threatening to boil over onto the stovetop. Just then, both the second phone line and the doorbell rang.

Overwhelmed, I could feel the old responses of rage and helplessness rising in my chest; I was ready to explode. Not knowing what else to do, I just quit. Took a deep breath and surrendered to Spirit. Almost immediately, this deep sense of peace replaced everything else. I don't know how long it lasted. Maybe a second, maybe a minute, maybe longer. I do know that as the waves of peacefulness moved through my being, Mateo stopped crying and laid his head on my shoulder. The answering machine took care of the phone. The lentils didn't boil over after all. And the mailman just left the package on our front porch and drove off. The incident passed, and I went on with my day. In that moment of surrender, nothing had changed, and yet everything had changed.

Please don't misunderstand. I'm not telling you this little story because I think it's important, or that what I did is special. To the contrary, it's just a snapshot of one moment in my life, which, with the exception of a few details, is probably not that much different from times in your life.

I've been meditating regularly for years. I've come to love those 20 to 30 minute blocks of quiet time, the Tai Chi and yoga sets, the journaling, the breathwork — and I suspect they'll always be an integral part of my life. But circumstances have changed in our household in the past year or so. Sometimes I go for several days without having the opportunity to sit for as long as I used to or to move as deeply inward as I would like. That's just the way it is, and it's not helpful to complain or wish it were otherwise. I've found that it is helpful for me to hold the intention to meditate whenever and wherever I am, for just as long as I can. Intention is the mother of manifestation. If I can just remember to hold the intention to find time and space to open mySelf to the Divine during the course of the day, it always seems to manifest. Sometimes it's an intense but brief experience, like that day in the kitchen. Sometimes it's softer and longer. It's not my job to judge my experience. I'm merely invited to stay focused on my willingness to open to the sweet flow of Spirit during all the little moments of my life, whenever they appear.

Meanwhile, I take heart in remembering the story of two young novice monks who were having trouble adjusting to life in the monastery. They were required to spend so much time in meditation that they could seldom smoke, so the one monk went to see the Abbot and asked, "Is it all right if I smoke during meditation?" to which the Abbot replied, "Absolutely not." So the second monk went to the Abbot and asked, "Is it all right if I meditate while smoking?" to which the Abbot smiled and said, "Yes, of course. It is good to meditate whenever you can."

I lack nothing —

except the awareness that I lack nothing.

In All Things Give Thanks

I'm often amazed by how well our five-month-old son, Mateo, can communicate his needs and desires without knowing or using words. For example, when autumn's first cold front moved into town two weeks ago, he clearly wanted to go outside immediately. Never mind that it was windy and drizzling. His little body could sense the change in atmosphere, and he made it known that he was being called outdoors. It was as if he'd been sent a personal invitation to attend a Big Party being thrown by Mother Nature. I resisted at first, because I could tell at a glance how cold it would be outside. But he would not be denied.

So, there we were, despite my initial misgivings, strolling through our neighborhood in the early morning hours. And we both loved it. The streets were slippery and demanded that we walk slowly, watching as our neighbors went scurrying between their houses and cars. We walked for a long time, then stopped for a rest under a particularly large pecan tree. Noticing that the sidewalk was covered with nuts that had been blown down by the rain, I quickly gathered a handful, and began shelling them. Having grown up with South Texas pecans, I think there's nothing quite like the taste of the first few pecans each year. What a feast of memories came with each bite of the new harvest!

Standing under that tree, sheltered from the drizzle

while munching pecans and holding my son in my arms, I experienced a flood of gratitude washing through my whole being. It was partly because of the joy of having Mateo's warm, loving body against mine on a cold day, feeling the miracle of his presence in our lives. It was partly the simple pleasure of being able to gather pecans so freely, appreciating that elsewhere on the planet these same tasty nuts are high-priced delicacies available only in gourmet food stores. It was partly the joy of feeling the first blasts of cold air after months of the humid heat in "Sauna-Antonio." But mostly it was that quiet euphoria flowing out of the awareness of my interconnectedness with all of Creation. The sudden knowing that this moment was made possible by all of the other moments that had preceded it in my life, the joyful ones and painful ones alike, much less the intricately woven web of life that contains trees, rain, neighbors, rivers and seasons. And this awareness filled me with such gratitude that it instantly seemed to fill my past, present and future with joy and wonder.

A cynical reader might ask, "So what? Why tell yet another baby story, Rudi? What's the big deal about feeling relaxed while walking in the rain?"

I don't claim to be unique. And certainly I'm not reporting anything new. Yet, in that moment, everything was so fresh and miraculous, reminding me to slow down and pay attention to my surroundings and to the very real miracles that are always present. Perhaps, as you read these words, you'll remember, too. And maybe, just maybe, the details of your life will flood you with gratitude. After all, Thanksgiving isn't just a day on the calendar — it's a way of being that calls to us throughout the year. In all things give thanks.

Being Grateful

Being grateful, you are almost too busy for anything else
tears well up, washing away old ghosts and shadows.

Being grateful, your mind is preoccupied
with more pressing matters
so, you have no need to locate a ladder
and try to get up to a higher spot,
you've got no time to entertain the door-to-door salesmen
peddling their shiny dreams of what might be if only, if only.
You're too busy to open junk mail or clean untidy drawers,
to put away dishes or answer yet another phone call.

Being grateful, you bite into an apple
and a waterfall of juice runs down your chin.
A thin wedge of salty cheese
reminds you of those two carefree weeks you spent
in the south of Spain way back when.
One single seedless grape causes an explosion
in the middle of your tongue,
and suddenly you're feeling very young again,
and logic doesn't matter quite as much
as you thought it did just a few moments earlier.

Being grateful, you are swallowed whole
and only your story remains.

Remembering the Reason

Driving through New Mexico last summer, I saw a gigantic double rainbow making two incredibly beautiful, vibrant arches from the desert floor to the top of a majestic mesa. Zet was fast asleep in the passenger seat at the time, and I didn't have the heart to wake her up, but I desperately wanted to share the experience with somebody, somehow. Keeping one eye on the road and one hand on the steering wheel, I grabbed pen and paper to scribble a few quick lines about this phenomenal sight. But even as I was writing the words, I knew it was an essentially futile gesture. Mere words wouldn't do the trick.

There I was, in the middle of a magical interplay of color, light and shadow, feeling overwhelmed by an awareness of transcendence. I just had to share or describe it to someone, but that was simply out of the question. Even now, months later, I distinctly remember the vastness and vivid colors of that rainbow, but I am painfully aware that these sentences are inadequate to the task of describing it — although that doesn't stop me from trying.

Similarly, it seems to me that the winter Holiday Season is basically about our deep-seated desire to remind ourselves and each other about the possibility of miracles, warmth and new life just as the cold sets in. It's almost as if we're collectively trying to show each other the shimmering rainbows hovering in the air. But it's so difficult to adequately describe in mere words the magical potential for new birth and new light in the heart of darkness.

Instead we have made up a number of stories, rituals and traditions to convey our culture's sense of wonder at this time of year. Since ancient times, priests and priestesses have invoked the power of the light during the Winter Solstice. As the Jewish Hanukkah tradition tells of oil lamps miraculously burning in the Temple without adequate fuel, the Christian story involves the virgin birth of a child surrounded by heavenly lights. Over the centuries, we have overlaid these stories with a rich tapestry of rituals and traditions, such as gift giving, feasting, sending greeting cards and decorating.

In recent years, it seems we've come to focus primarily on these traditions and rituals, often forgetting what it is we're really trying to say to each other underneath these outer trappings. We as a society have a strong need to remember the underlying Reason for the Season, to connect with the Light at the beginning of winter, to remind ourselves and each other of the power of the Spirit alive in the world in the face of all the seeming evidence to the contrary.

On the other hand, as I discovered with my rainbow experience, it's not really all that useful to use words to describe miracles. It's more about bearing witness to them by acting, smiling, touching, listening, giving and receiving from a place of remembering who you truly are, today and every day.

Receiving Your Present

This gift isn't really mine to give, but I'm doing my best to give it to you anyway, in hopes that you'll take a few minutes out of your busy life to receive it consciously. If you aren't sitting down as you read these words, please take a few moments to do so now. Make yourself as comfortable as possible, ready to accept delivery and unwrap this gift slowly and carefully, like the fragile treasure it is.

The Precious Present is nothing more (but nothing less) than this very moment unfolding all of its riches in your life right now. It's PRECIOUS because it is priceless, irreplaceable and incredibly valuable. It's PRESENT because it's happening at this very moment; it has never happened before in the history of the world, and will never ever occur precisely like this again. Our culture has hypnotized many of us into believing that our minutes, days and years stretch out in a straight line of identical, measurable units which can be scheduled, planned and interchanged at will. The Precious Present proves otherwise.

That's because it asks us to be still for a while. To drop the illusion of linear life long enough to breathe fully, sit quietly and drink in the miracle of our connection to all of life. It is inviting you now. So just keep breathing, reading with an open and relaxed mind, focusing on the heart of this Precious Present. You know exactly what it is. You've always known. You're just taking a moment to remember two simple facts: 1) you are precious, and 2) you are present. Slowly, gradually, these two facts melt into the one awareness that is the Precious Present.

Just sitting here comfortably, without doing a single other thing except opening up to this moment, you may find yourself caught up in a flurry of feelings, fantasies, plans and prayers. That's okay. Just be kind to yourself. Remind yourself gently that you have a very Precious Present waiting for you, right here, right now.

This is not a new gift by any means. It's been offered by many other writers and teachers over the years. It's also been beautifully described in *The Precious Present*, a wonderfully poetic little book by Spencer Johnson. Zet gave me a copy many years ago and it's one of my all-time favorites.

The nice thing about the Precious Present is that you can give it to others — or to yourself — anytime, again and again. Like right now. Or, if you've got other things to do now, you can just set it aside and come back to it later, whenever you're ready. There's no need to hurry. Enjoy!

Ten Allowances
Guidelines for Living from the Inside Out

1. Allow yourself time to listen. Sitting still and focusing directly on Deep Silence works — but so does focusing on your breath and/or a flower, rock, river, cloud, or candle. Miracles happen in the silent spaces between your thoughts and your senses.

2. Allow yourself to connect with your Purpose in life. You may find it helpful to define your personal Statement of Purpose as succinctly as possible, then focus on it on a regular basis.

3. Allow yourself to follow your intuition. Your intuition is central to staying on course and living a life that truly fits you. (Hint: it requires listening. See #1 above.)

4. Allow yourself good food and drink. There's no need to get rigid about it, but your Body Temple simply functions better when it is being fed the optimum fuel.

5. Allow yourself time to do what you love to do as frequently as possible. Don't wait until that Magic Someday when you will have enough time. Start now. Don't try to "make time" or "take time" to do what you love; simply *allow* time for it. You deserve it!

6. Allow yourself to notice what you really "hate" to do — then do it anyway with as much love as you can muster. You'll be surprised what gifts your "dislikes" have for you, if you'll welcome them instead of trying to push them away.

7. Allow yourself to "fail" the tests and temptations occasionally. There will *always* be tests. Some you'll pass with flying colors; some you'll think you failed miserably. But the Good News is that these are usually open book tests. Spirit makes sure you already know the answers before you're tested. It's just up to you to stop, look and listen with your heart. (See #1 again....)

8. Allow yourself to associate with other people who are committed to living from the inside out. Birds of a feather succeed together! Do your best to hang out with, give to, buy or barter from people who are doing/selling what they truly love. You'll be amazed to discover how many people are eager to support you in doing what you love, particularly when you've consciously chosen to support others in doing the same. Quality counts.

9. Allow it to be easy. By definition, Living from the Inside Out is easy. If what you're doing feels too hard, it probably is. Stop as soon as possible. Then just sit and be still. (Remember #1!) Wait until the feeling of struggle passes and is replaced with ease and well-being. Nobody said life would always feel fun. However, there's really no reason why most things can't feel peaceful, if you're willing to give up your need to be right all the time.

10. Allow yourself to enjoy the process of remembering your path. It's important not to beat yourself up when you forget and/or lose your way. If it seems like you've gotten off track, let yourself feel good about the fact that you've remembered. What you focus on expands — so you might as well have fun focusing on what you love. Why not?

Blessings

May your feet take you places where your heart will thrive
alive with the tastes of adventure.

May your heart stay open and your mind stay clear.
May you embrace the ones you love
and make peace with what you fear.

May you make your choices wisely
and make the best of what you get.

May you encounter all the love you desire,
all the things you need,
and all the dreams you can accommodate
in the mansion of your heart.

Acknowledgements

Thanks to all the teachers and students who have taught me so many valuable lessons over the years. I'm especially grateful to my friend and mentor Arnold M. Patent, whose clear and patient explanations of Universal Principles have helped me explore the practical applications of spirituality in daily life. And to Mary Manin Morrissey for courageously modeling the powerful process of "living your dream."

Thanks, also, to the good folks in the Celebration Circle of San Antonio for their unconditional love and support over the years. They have been very gracious in allowing me to experiment with various ways of exploring and expressing my questions. Many of the writings in this book initially came to life as talks shared during our Sunday morning gatherings or in columns written for the Circle newsletter.

I'm also grateful to the kind people who have pointedly and repeatedly urged me to publish my reflections in a book such as this. And I'm particularly grateful to Shirley Durst for having initiated the process of collecting, editing and shepherding this project toward completion. Without her, this would still be just another good idea waiting to happen.

This said, my deepest appreciation goes to my parents, my children, Mateo and Sarah, and especially, to Zet Baer, my best friend and wife of many years. I have drawn freely from the bottomless well of goodness provided by our home and family — and I *know* I have been blessed.

More of Rudi Harst's encouraging words and music are available on the following tapes and CDs:

Now and Then A sparkling collection of contemporary acoustic music. Enjoy 12 of Rudi's original songs presented in an engaging variety of musical styles and rhythms, including *Shoulda, Coulda, Woulda and It's All in Your Mind.*

CD $15.00 / CASSETTE $10.00

Peace, Be Still A very gentle and effective guided meditation, ideal for novices and experienced meditators alike. This rich blend of Rudi's soothing spoken words, singing and acoustic guitar instrumentals creates a compelling pathway to inner peace.

CD $15.00

What's Your Story This thought-provoking tape contains a series of four talks in which Rudi examines the process of naming and claiming the power of your story.

CASSETTE $10.00

These products, as well as additional copies of this book, can be ordered from:

Celebration Circle Publishing
1830 East Pyron
San Antonio, TX 78223
circle@celebrationcircle.org

To learn more about the ongoing work of the Celebration Circle or inquire about Rudi's availability as a speaker, workshop presenter and performance artist, please visit the Circle website:

www.celebrationcircle.org